The Perfect Christmas

The Perfect
Christmas

This edition published in 2011

LOVE FOOD is an imprint of Parragon Books Ltd

Parragon
Queen Street House
4 Queen Street
Bath BA1 1HE, UK

ISBN: 978-1-4454-3429-2
Printed in China

Introduction by Dominic Utton
New recipes written by Sandra Baddeley
Cover design by Donna-Marie Scrase and Talking Design
Design by Donna-Marie Scrase
Cover photography and additional photography by Clive Streeter
Cover food styling by Teresa Goldfinch
Additional food styling by Angela Drake

Notes for the Reader
This book uses both metric and imperial measurements. Follow the same units of measurement throughout; do not mix metric and imperial. All spoon measurements are level: teaspoons are assumed to be 5 ml, and tablespoons are assumed to be 15 ml. Unless otherwise stated, milk is assumed to be full fat, eggs and individual vegetables are medium, and pepper is freshly ground black pepper.

The times given are an approximate guide only. Preparation times differ according to the techniques used by different people and the cooking times may also vary from those given. Optional ingredients, variations or serving suggestions have not been included in the calculations.

Recipes using raw or very lightly cooked eggs should be avoided by infants, the elderly, pregnant women, convalescents and anyone suffering from an illness. Pregnant and breastfeeding women are advised to avoid eating peanuts and peanut products. Sufferers from nut allergies should be aware that some of the ready-made ingredients used in the recipes in this book may contain nuts. Always check the packaging before use.

CONTENTS

INTRODUCTION

E verybody has an image of the perfect Christmas. Snowflakes and roaring fires, steam puddings, golden turkeys and the glitter of tinsel on the tree. Presents and laughter and family and tradition. All of the things that make those few days at the end of December, as Andy Williams sang, 'the most wonderful time of the year'.

Christmas should be wonderful – not stressful, or time consuming, or even terribly expensive. With a little planning, a touch of creativity and a healthy sprinkle of seasonal spirit, making your yuletide a time of real magic can be something even the busiest and most budget-conscious family can achieve.

THE FIVE RULES OF CHRISTMAS

Storage

The key to simplicity lies in careful planning. And that starts – believe it or not – the moment you take down last year's decorations. Store everything in clearly labelled shoeboxes and old sweet tins – and keep them all together in another box in the attic. For tangle-free lights, cut a rectangle of strong cardboard, make a slot in one end and feed the string of lights into it, securing with sticky tape. Then simply wrap the lights around the cardboard, cutting another slot in the other end to secure the plug. A bit of bubble wrap around the lot and they're ready for next year!

Budgeting

Newsflash: Christmas is expensive! December is not an ordinary month, and you shouldn't expect your pay packet to have to cope as though it is. Be realistic

– keep all your receipts this year, tot them up and divide the total by 11: that's the amount you have to save each month next year in order to make Christmas pay for itself. Remember – if you can't afford a little amount regularly, how on earth can you justify spending it all in one go?

Shopping

Easy one this: buy your cards in January when they're cheap. Think ahead where presents are concerned – there is no rule which says Christmas gifts have to be bought in the weeks before Christmas. Be realistic about how much food and drink you actually need – and try not to overestimate the turkey again! Think 450 g/1 lb per person plus another 450 g/1 lb for luck and you won't go too far wrong.

Party season

Everyone over-indulges at Christmas. There's the official office party, the unofficial (better) office party, drinks at the neighbours, nights out with friends, visits from family… So what do you want us to tell you? There is no magic hangover cure, sadly! But try to remember not to drink so quickly, or eat too much rich food; try to alternate alcohol with soft drinks and always have plenty of water before bed. Good luck!

Spread the load

Of course you want to make the season special for your family… but it's important to remember that you're a member of the family too. Every Santa needs his helpers: make a list of jobs and divide them up. Don't look on it as necessary chores, but rather a series of fun activities that should, whenever possible, be shared. Get a festive CD on, throw a bit of tinsel around and enjoy yourselves – it's Christmas!

COUNTDOWN TO CHRISTMAS TIME PLANNER

By Spring
- Compile all festive recipes and make a note of their location in your calendar.
- Shop around for cheap card and decoration deals.

By early Summer
- Begin compiling a gift list and shop for bargains when they appear.
- Bookmark any useful websites for gift and decoration ideas.

By late September
- Organise your address book and make sure it is up-to-date.
- Finalise any travel plans and, where possible, book tickets in advance.

By November
- Organise all festive events in your calendar.
- Buy stamps and any extra cards.
- Print or order any photos you want to include in your cards.
- Shop for decoration/ craft supplies.

By early December
- Get out decorations and check lights.
- Make food shopping list and clear space in the freezer.
- Post gifts and write cards.

By mid December
- Post all cards.
- Decorate tree and wrap presents.
- Finish all food and gift shopping – including the turkey!

December 18th
- Check and recheck all gifts and food.

Christmas Eve

- Defrost the turkey – allow 2 hours per kg (1 kg equals 2 lb 4 oz). When it is fully thawed, store in the fridge overnight.
- Pre-cook the roast potatoes and parsnips.

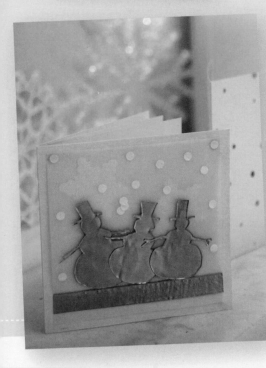

Christmas Day

These timings are correct for a 4 kg/9 lb turkey. Adjust cooking times for bigger/smaller birds! Cooking times can be calculated simply by remembering the following rules: if it's less than 4 kg/9 lb, then allow 20 minutes per 1 kg/2 lb 4 oz plus another 70 minutes. If it's 4 kg/9 lb or more, cook for 20 minutes per 1 kg/2 lb 4 oz plus another 90 minutes.

- 8.00 am – Take the turkey from the fridge and leave to come to room temperature.
- 10.00 – Preheat the oven to 190°C/375°F/ Gas Mark 5.
- 10.40 – Start cooking the turkey, as per recipe.
- 1.00 pm – Put Christmas pudding in to steam. Open the red wine to breathe or chill some white wine. Put sausages and bacon rolls into the oven and cook for about 45 minutes until crisp.
    - 1.30 – Check the turkey is cooked, remove from oven and wrap in foil. Make the gravy.
    - 1.50 – Place pre-cooked roast potatoes into the hot oven.
    - 2.10 – Add pre-cooked parsnips to the potatoes. Heat serving dishes and plates.
    - 2.20 – Cook Brussels sprouts.
    - 2.30 – Take a moment out for a well-deserved glass of wine!
    - 2.45 – Carve the turkey.
    - 3.00 – Enjoy the rest of the day!

1

Traditional
FAVOURITES

A Traditional
CHRISTMAS

Tradition is at the heart of Christmas. Despite the increasing commercialisation of the season, real Yuletide magic comes from tapping into traditions centuries old. Every year, when we open the doors of our advent calendars, kiss under the mistletoe, decorate the tree and write Christmas cards, we're simply following in the great traditions of Christmases past.

The Christmas tree, for example, has its origins in 16th-century Germany, when people would decorate fir trees with apples, candles and coloured paper in celebration of the season. Christmas cards first came about in the 18th century, when children would show off their writing skills to their parents on Christmas Day – but became a national (then international) phenomenon after the introduction of the 'Penny Post' in 1840.

Father Christmas may now appear straight out of Disney central casting, but the essential idea – that of an old man with a sack of gifts – has been around for 1700 years. St Nicholas of Myra (now modern-day Turkey) was a fourth-century Christian leader who gave money anonymously to the poor every December. According to legend, he would drop coins down the chimney, into stockings that had been hung up to dry.

But, perhaps oddly, there is one tradition still practised today that's actually older than Christmas itself. Two hundred years before the birth of Christ, Druids in northern Europe used mistletoe as the centrepiece of their winter celebrations: the plant was believed to have magical healing properties. In Scandinavia it was also the symbol for the goddess of love – hence the modern practice of kissing under the mistletoe!

Some traditions, of course, remain peculiar to one's own family: and what better way to come together than to create a craft project – in this case, to make Christmas snowflake cards. For this project, you will need scissors, a pencil, craft knife, steel-edged ruler, cutting mat, masking tape, bone folder, double-sided tape, old newspaper, face mask and protective gloves.

Christmas Snowflake Cards

Materials

- card 3 mm/⅛ inch thick
- 300 gsm Bockingford (slightly textured) paper
- 300 gsm white card
- silver and/or gold spray paint
- silver and/or gold card
- craft equipment (see bottom of page 12)

1 Enlarge the template on page 220 on a photocopier as directed and cut out with scissors. Draw around the template on to the 3-mm/⅛-inch thick card and cut out with a craft knife and steel-edged ruler on a cutting mat.

2 Place the template on the Bockingford paper and secure with masking tape. Ensure there is enough space to create a 15-cm/6-inch square. Turn the paper over and rub firmly all over the template area with a bone folder to create an impression.

3 Remove the template. Ensure that the embossed snowflake is in the centre of the paper, then trim to 15 cm/6 inches square.

4 Cut a piece of white card 15 x 30 cm/ 6 x 12 inches. Score down the centre with a bone folder and fold in half. Use double-sided tape around the edges of the embossed snowflake panel to attach it to the card.

5 Repeat steps 2 to 4 to create a second card, but adhere the Bockingford paper to the opposite side of the white card to create a reversed impression.

6 To make a third card, place the template on the front of the folded white card (see step 4). Protect your work surface with old newspaper. Wearing a face mask and protective gloves, spray silver and/or gold paint over the card. When dry, remove the template to reveal the snowflake.

7 To make a fourth card, cut a piece of silver or gold card 15 x 30 cm/ 6 x 12 inches. Score down the centre with a bone folder and fold in half. Respray the snowflake template so that it contrasts with the card, if needed, and attach it to the card front with double-sided tape.

Traditional Roast
TURKEY

Serves 8

- 1 quantity Chestnut & Sausage
  Stuffing (see page 94)
- a 5-kg/11-lb turkey
- 40 g/1½ oz butter
- bread sauce, to serve 8
  (see page 30)
- roast potatoes, to serve 8
  (see page 16)
- spiced winter vegetables,
  to serve 8 (see page 90)
- bay and sage leaves,
  to garnish

1 Preheat the oven to 220°C/425°F/Gas Mark 7. Spoon one quantity of Chestnut & Sausage Stuffing into the neck cavity of the turkey and close the flap of skin with a skewer. Place the bird in a large roasting tin and rub it all over with the butter. Roast in the preheated oven for 1 hour, then lower the oven temperature to 180°C/350°F/Gas Mark 4 and roast for a further 2½ hours. You may need to pour off the fat from the roasting tin occasionally.

2 Check that the turkey is cooked by inserting a skewer or the point of a sharp knife into the thigh – if the juices run clear, it is ready. Transfer the bird to a carving board, cover loosely with foil and leave to rest.

3 Garnish the turkey with bay and sage leaves. Carve and serve with the warm bread sauce, roast potatoes and vegetables.

Perfect Roast
POTATOES

....

Serves 8

- 70 g/2½ oz goose or duck
  fat or 5 tbsp olive oil
- 1 kg/2 lb 4 oz even-sized
  potatoes, peeled
- coarse sea salt
- 8 fresh rosemary sprigs,
  to garnish

1 Preheat the oven to 230°C/450°F/Gas Mark 8. Put the fat in a large roasting tin, sprinkle generously with sea salt and place in the preheated oven.

2 Meanwhile, cook the potatoes in a large saucepan of boiling water for 8–10 minutes until par-boiled. Drain well and, if the potatoes are large, cut them in half. Return the potatoes to the empty saucepan and shake vigorously to roughen their outsides.

3 Arrange the potatoes in a single layer in the hot fat and roast for 45 minutes. If they look as if they are beginning to char around the edges, reduce the oven temperature to 200°C/400°F/Gas Mark 6. Turn the potatoes over and roast for a further 30 minutes until crisp. Serve garnished with rosemary sprigs.

Rich Christmas
PUDDING

- 200 g/7 oz currants
- 200 g/7 oz raisins
- 200 g/7 oz sultanas
- 150 ml/5 fl oz sweet sherry
- 175 g/6 oz butter, plus extra for greasing
- 175 g/6 oz brown sugar
- 4 eggs, beaten
- 150 g/5½ oz self-raising flour
- 100 g/3½ oz fresh white or wholemeal breadcrumbs
- 50 g/1¾ oz blanched almonds, chopped
- juice of 1 orange
- grated rind of ½ orange
- grated rind of ½ lemon
- ½ tsp mixed spice
- holly, to decorate
- icing sugar, for dusting

Cook's note...

If you have too much of the mixture and it fills the pudding basin, it is a good idea to make a pleat across the centre of the first greaseproof paper and foil rounds, to allow plenty of room for the pudding to expand during cooking.

1 Put the currants, raisins and sultanas in a glass bowl and pour the sherry over. Cover and leave to soak for at least 2 hours.

2 Beat together the butter and brown sugar in a bowl. Beat in the eggs, then fold in the flour. Stir in the soaked fruit and the sherry with the breadcrumbs, almonds, orange juice and rind, lemon rind and mixed spice. Grease a 1.2-litre/2-pint pudding basin and spoon the mixture into it, packing it down well and leaving a gap of 2.5 cm/1 inch at the top. Cut a round of greaseproof paper 3 cm/1¼ inches larger than the top of the basin, grease with butter and place over the pudding. Secure with string, then top with two layers of foil. Place the pudding in a saucepan filled with boiling water that reaches two-thirds of the way up the basin. Reduce the heat and simmer for 6 hours, topping up the water in the saucepan when necessary.

3 Remove from the heat and leave to cool. Renew the greaseproof paper and foil and store in the refrigerator for 2–8 weeks. To reheat, steam as before for 2 hours. Decorate with holly and a dusting of icing sugar.

Festive
MINCE PIES

Serves 16

- 200 g/7 oz plain flour, plus extra for dusting
- 100 g/3½ oz butter, plus extra for greasing
- 25 g/1 oz icing sugar
- 1 egg yolk
- 2–3 tbsp milk, plus extra for glazing
- 300 g/10½ oz mincemeat
- icing sugar, for dusting

Cook's note...

To make your own mincemeat, mix together 450 g/1 lb mixed dried fruit, 115 g/4 oz demerara sugar, 115 g/4 oz shredded suet, 115 g/4 oz mixed peel, 115 g/4 oz chopped blanched almonds, finely grated rind and juice of 1 lemon, 115 g/4 oz grated apple, 1 teaspoon mixed spice, ½ teaspoon freshly grated nutmeg, ½ teaspoon ground cinnamon and 4 tablespoons brandy. Pack into sterilized jars and seal the lids.

1 Preheat the oven to 180°C/350°F/Gas Mark 4. Grease a 16-hole tart tin with butter. Sift the flour into a bowl. Using your fingertips, rub in the remaining butter until the mixture resembles breadcrumbs. Stir in the sugar and egg yolk. Stir in enough milk to make a soft dough, turn out on to a lightly floured work surface and knead lightly until smooth.

2 Shape the dough into a ball and roll out to a thickness of 1 cm/½ inch. Use fluted cutters to cut out 10 rounds measuring 7 cm/2¾ inches in diameter and use to line the holes in the prepared tart tin. Half-fill each pie with mincemeat. Cut out 16 star shapes from the leftover dough, brush with milk and place on top of each pie.

3 Glaze the surface with more milk and bake in the preheated oven for 15 minutes until the pastry is a pale golden colour. Remove from the oven and leave to cool in the tin. Dust with icing sugar before serving.

Christmas
CAKE

....

Makes a 20-cm/8-inch cake

- 150 g/5½ oz raisins
- 125 g/4½ oz dried dates, stoned and chopped
- 125 g/4½ oz sultanas
- 100 g/3½ oz glacé cherries, rinsed
- 150 ml/5 fl oz brandy
- 225 g/8 oz butter, plus extra for greasing
- 200 g/7 oz caster sugar
- 4 eggs

- grated rind of 1 orange
- grated rind of 1 lemon
- 1 tbsp black treacle
- 225 g/8 oz plain flour
- ½ tsp salt
- ½ tsp baking powder
- 1 tsp mixed spice
- 25 g/1 oz toasted almonds, chopped

- 25 g/1 oz toasted hazelnuts, chopped
- 750 g/1 lb 10 oz marzipan
- 3 tbsp apricot jam, warmed
- 3 egg whites
- 650 g/1 lb 7 oz icing sugar
- edible silver balls and ribbon, to decorate

1 Make this cake at least 3 weeks in advance. Put all the fruit in a bowl and pour over the brandy. Cover and leave to soak overnight.

2 Preheat the oven to 110°C/225°F/Gas Mark ¼. Grease a 20-cm/8-inch cake tin with butter and line it with greaseproof paper. Cream the remaining butter and the caster sugar in a bowl until fluffy. Gradually beat in the eggs. Stir in the citrus rind and treacle. Sift the flour, salt, baking powder and mixed spice into a separate bowl, then fold into the egg mixture. Fold in the soaked fruit and brandy and the nuts, then spoon the mixture into the prepared cake tin.

3 Bake in the preheated oven for at least 3 hours. If it browns too quickly, cover with foil. The cake is cooked when a skewer inserted into the centre comes out clean. Remove from the oven and leave to cool on a wire rack. Store in an airtight container until required.

4 Roll out the marzipan and cut to shape to cover the top and sides of the cake. Brush the cake with the jam and press the marzipan on to the surface. Make the icing by placing the egg whites in a bowl and adding the icing sugar a little at a time, beating well until the icing is very thick and will stand up in peaks. Spread over the covered cake, using a fork to give texture. Decorate as you wish with silver balls and ribbon.

STOLLEN

Serves 10

- 85 g/3 oz currants
- 55 g/2 oz raisins
- 35 g/1¼ oz mixed peel, chopped
- 55 g/2 oz glacé cherries, rinsed, dried and quartered
- 2 tbsp dark rum
- 4 tbsp butter
- 175 ml/6 fl oz milk
- 3 tbsp golden caster sugar
- 375 g/13 oz strong white flour, plus extra for dusting
- ½ tsp salt
- ½ tsp ground nutmeg
- ½ tsp ground cinnamon
- seeds from 3 cardamom pods
- 2 tsp easy-blend dried yeast
- finely grated rind of 1 lemon
- 1 egg, beaten
- 40 g/1½ oz flaked almonds
- oil, for greasing
- 175 g/6 oz marzipan
- melted butter, for brushing
- icing sugar, for dusting

1 Put the currants, raisins, mixed peel and cherries in a bowl. Stir in the rum and set aside. Put the butter, milk and caster sugar in a saucepan and heat gently until the sugar has dissolved and the butter has just melted. Sift the flour, salt, nutmeg and cinnamon into a bowl. Crush the cardamom seeds and add them to the flour mixture. Stir in the yeast. Make a well in the centre and stir in the milk mixture, lemon rind and egg. Beat to form a soft dough.

2 Turn out the dough onto a floured work surface. With floured hands, knead the dough for about 5 minutes. It will be quite sticky, so add more flour if necessary. Knead the soaked fruit and flaked almonds into the dough until just combined. Place the dough in a clean, lightly oiled bowl. Cover with clingfilm and leave in a warm place for 1½ hours, or until doubled in size. Turn out the dough onto a floured work surface and knead lightly for 1–2 minutes, then roll out to a 25-cm/10-inch square.

3 Roll the marzipan into a sausage shape slightly shorter than the length of the dough and place down the centre. Fold one side over to cover the marzipan. Repeat with the other side, overlapping in the centre. Seal the ends. Place the roll, seam-side down, on a greased baking sheet. Cover with oiled clingfilm and leave in a warm place until doubled in size. Preheat the oven to 190°C/375°F/ Gas Mark 5. Bake the stollen for 40 minutes, or until golden. Brush the hot stollen generously with melted butter and dredge heavily with icing sugar.

Festive Sherry
TRIFLE

Serves 4–6

- 100 g/3½ oz trifle sponges
- raspberry jam, for spreading
- 150 ml/5 fl oz sherry
- 150 g/5½ oz frozen raspberries, thawed
- 350 g/12 oz fresh strawberries, sliced

Custard layer

- 6 egg yolks
- 50 g/1¾ oz caster sugar
- 500 ml/18 fl oz milk
- 1 tsp vanilla extract

Topping

- 300 ml/10 fl oz double cream
- 1–2 tbsp caster sugar
- 1 chocolate bar, crumbled

1 Spread the trifle sponges with jam, cut them into bite-sized cubes and arrange in the bottom of a large glass serving bowl. Pour over the sherry and leave to stand for 30 minutes.

2 Combine the raspberries and strawberries and spoon them over the sponges in the bowl.

3 To make the custard, put the egg yolks and sugar into a bowl and whisk together. Pour the milk into a saucepan and warm gently over a low heat. Remove from the heat and gradually stir into the egg mixture, then return the mixture to the saucepan and stir constantly over a low heat until thickened. Do not boil. Remove from the heat, pour into a bowl and stir in the vanilla. Leave to cool for 1 hour. Spread the custard over the trifle, cover with clingfilm and chill in the refrigerator for 2 hours.

4 To make the topping, whip the cream in a bowl and stir in the sugar to taste. Spread the cream over the trifle, and then scatter over the chocolate pieces. Chill in the refrigerator for 30 minutes before serving.

Sugar-glazed
PARSNIPS

Serves 8

- 24 small parsnips, chopped
- about 1 tsp salt
- 115 g/4 oz butter
- 115 g/4 oz soft brown sugar

Cook's note...

When buying parsnips, look for firm roots with no rusty patches and no damage to the skin. Store them in a cool, well-ventilated place for up to 5 days. Try to buy parsnips that are all about the same size, for even cooking.

1 Place the parsnips in a saucepan, add just enough water to cover, then add the salt. Bring to the boil, reduce the heat, cover and simmer for 20–25 minutes, until tender. Drain well.

2 Melt the butter in a heavy-based pan or wok. Add the parsnips and toss well. Sprinkle with the sugar, then cook, stirring constantly to prevent the sugar from sticking to the pan or burning.

3 Cook the parsnips for 10–15 minutes, until golden and glazed. Transfer to a warmed serving dish and serve immediately.

Sage, Onion & Apple
STUFFING

Serves 10

- 550 g/1 lb 4 oz pork sausage meat
- 1 onion, grated
- 350 g/12 oz cooking apple, peeled, cored and finely chopped
- 25 g/1 oz fresh white breadcrumbs
- 2 tbsp chopped fresh sage or marjoram
- grated rind of 1 lemon
- 1 egg, beaten
- sage sprig, to garnish

1 Preheat the oven to 200°C/400°F/Gas Mark 6. Place the sausage meat, onion, 300g/10½ oz of the cooking apple, breadcrumbs, sage or marjoram, lemon rind and egg in a large bowl and mix together until thoroughly combined.

2 Sprinkle the sausage mixture with the reserved chopped apple and then place in a 900 g/2 lb loaf tin or shape into balls.

3 Bake in the preheated oven for 50 minutes, until the apple is golden and the sausage meat is cooked through. Garnish with a sprig of sage and serve immediately.

Bread
SAUCE

Serves 12

- 1 onion, peeled but left whole
- 12 cloves
- 1 bay leaf
- 6 peppercorns
- 600 ml/1 pint milk
- 115 g/4 oz fresh white breadcrumbs
- 25 g/1 oz butter
- ½ tsp grated nutmeg
- 2 tbsp double cream (optional)
- salt and pepper

1 Make 12 small holes in the onion using a skewer and stick a clove in each hole.

2 Place the onion, bay leaf and peppercorns in a small saucepan and pour in the milk. Place over a medium heat, bring to the boil, remove from the heat, then cover and leave to infuse for 1 hour.

3 Strain the milk and discard the onion, bay leaf and peppercorns.

4 Return the milk to the rinsed-out saucepan and add the breadcrumbs. Cook the sauce over a very gentle heat until the breadcrumbs have swollen and the sauce is thick. Beat in the butter and season well to taste.

5 When ready to serve, reheat the sauce briefly, if necessary. Add the nutmeg and stir in the double cream, if using. Pour into a warmed serving bowl and serve with the turkey.

Christmas Onion
GRAVY

Serves 8

- 30 ml sunflower oil
- 450 g/1 lb onions, thinly sliced
- 2 garlic cloves, crushed
- 1 tbsp sugar
- 25 g/1 oz plain flour
- 150 ml/5 fl oz red wine
- 600 ml/1 pint boiling beef or vegetable stock
- 2 tsp Dijon mustard
- ⅛ tsp gravy browning (optional)
- salt and pepper

1 Heat the oil in a large, heavy-based saucepan. Add the onions, garlic and sugar and fry over a low heat for 30 minutes, stirring occasionally, until very soft and light golden.

2 Stir in the flour and cook for 1 minute. Add the red wine and bring to the boil, then simmer and beat until the mixture is smooth. Add 150 ml/5 fl oz of the stock and return the mixture to the boil. Simmer and beat again to mix thoroughly.

3 Stir in the remaining stock, Dijon mustard and gravy browning, if using. Return the mixture to the boil once more and season to taste.

4 Simmer for 20 minutes and serve hot.

Cranberry
SAUCE

- thinly pared rind and juice of 1 lemon
- thinly pared rind and juice of 1 orange
- 350 g/12 oz cranberries, thawed if frozen
- 140 g/5 oz caster sugar
- 2 tbsp arrowroot, mixed with 3 tbsp cold water

1 Cut the strips of lemon and orange rind into thin shreds and place in a heavy-based saucepan. If using fresh cranberries, rinse well and remove any stalks. Add the berries, citrus juice and sugar to the saucepan and cook over a medium heat, stirring occasionally, for 5 minutes, or until the berries begin to burst.

2 Strain the juice into a clean saucepan and reserve the cranberries. Stir the arrowroot mixture into the juice, then bring to the boil, stirring constantly, until the sauce is smooth and thickened. Remove from the heat and stir in the reserved cranberries.

3 Transfer the cranberry sauce to a bowl and leave to cool, then cover with clingfilm and chill in the refrigerator.

2
Drinks &
APPETIZERS

In The Christmas
SPIRIT

Not for nothing is Christmas known as the party season. If the big day itself is all about family, then the weeks building up to the 25th can be a social whirlwind – and the chances are you're going to find yourself playing host at some stage this December.

But whether you're simply having a few friends over for drinks, entertaining the neighbours with some nibbles, or throwing a full-on dinner bash, showing a little seasonal goodwill need not become an organisational nightmare.

First things first. The golden rule of any gathering is not to run out of food and drink. Always prepare more than you think you'll need – and remember the all-important 'bring a bottle' line on the invitation! For those not super-confident in their nibble-making abilities (or the teetotal) it can also be fun to suggest some guests bring their own culinary creations. Otherwise, tons of ideas for simple appetizers and drinks can be found in this chapter.

Make – or buy – some Christmas compilation CDs and have them playing as your guests arrive. Even if they're not exactly the dancing types, a little festive music will do wonders to put people in the mood – and cover any early awkward silences.

And, of course, set the scene. It's Christmas – and this is a Christmas party! So decorate appropriately. Mistletoe may seem a bit hackneyed – but a sprig over the door is still a good ice-breaker. A few well-placed poinsettias can add a lovely rich, warm glow to a room – and for a real rustic sense of Christmases past, see the next page for an easy, effective Country-style garland that should provide a striking centrepiece for any gathering. For this project, you will need scissors, tailor's chalk, a craft knife, cutting mat, tape measure, fabric glue, long-nosed pliers, strong double-sided tape and thin craft wire.

Country-style Garland

Materials

- 1 small-weave and 1 large-weave hessian fabric, both 30-cm/12 inches square
- scraps of pale-green and deep-red felt
- red gingham and red cotton scraps
- natural string
- decorative gold fine thread or ribbon
- 5 red buttons, 2 cm/¾ inch in diameter
- needle and red thread
- 6 tiny wooden pegs
- 2 tiny felt hearts
- craft equipment (see bottom of page 36)

1 Enlarge the templates on page 220 on a photocopier as directed and cut out using scissors. Using tailor's chalk and either scissors or a craft knife on a cutting mat, cut out the following: 2 circles from small-weave hessian, 2 from large-weave hessian; 2 large stars from each hessian, 1 small star from green felt; 4 angel bodies from large-weave hessian; 4 angel wings from small-weave hessian; 2 large hearts from red gingham, 2 from plain red; 2 small hearts from red gingham, 2 from plain red, 2 from green felt.

2 Lay a 1.5 m/59-inch length of string on a work surface and twist the gold thread around. Tie a loop at either end and fray the ends.

3 Cover one side of each button with fabric glue and adhere to the red felt. Cut around the buttons with a craft knife. Pass the needle and thread through the buttonholes once so the thread ends dangle from the back of the button by about 1.5 cm/⅝ inch. Ensure two of the buttons have extra thread hanging.

4 Arrange the embellishments on the string, working out from the centre. Run a length of thin wire around the top of the red and gingham large hearts with pliers and use double-sided tape to sandwich between the fabrics. Glue a small green heart to the plain red side and add one of the buttons. Use two pegs to attach to the string.

5 Construct the angels in the same way, but simply sandwich the string in between the head and tops of the wings. Sandwich the wings (two sets per angel) in between the bodies. Glue the tiny felt hearts in place.

6 Construct the remaining embellishments in the same way, using wire to strengthen them, and attach to the string.

37

Wild Mushroom &
SHERRY SOUP

Serves 4
- 2 tbsp olive oil
- 1 onion, chopped
- 1 garlic clove, chopped
- 125 g/4½ oz sweet potato, peeled and chopped
- 1 leek, trimmed and sliced
- 200 g/7 oz button and chestnut mushrooms
- 150 g/5½ oz mixed wild mushrooms
- 600 ml/1 pint vegetable stock
- 350 ml/12 fl oz single cream
- 4 tbsp dry sherry
- salt and pepper

Cook's note...
An increasing range of wild mushrooms is now available in supermarkets. If fresh ones are not available, use 40–55 g/1½–2 oz dried instead. Soak them in hot water for 30 minutes and drain well before using.

To garnish
- Parmesan cheese shavings
- sautéed wild mushrooms, sliced

1 Heat the oil in a saucepan over a medium heat. Add the onion and garlic and cook, stirring, for 3 minutes, until slightly soft. Add the sweet potato and cook, stirring, for 3 minutes. Add the leek and cook, stirring, for 2 minutes.

2 Stir in the mushrooms, stock and cream. Bring to the boil, then reduce the heat and simmer gently, stirring occasionally, for 25 minutes. Remove from the heat, stir in the sherry and leave to cool slightly.

3 Transfer half the soup to a food processor and blend until smooth. Return the mixture to the saucepan with the rest of the soup, season to taste and reheat gently, stirring. Pour into four warmed soup bowls and garnish with Parmesan cheese shavings and sautéed wild mushrooms.

Spiced
PUMPKIN SOUP

....

Serves 4

- 2 tbsp olive oil
- 1 onion, chopped
- 1 garlic clove, chopped
- 1 tbsp chopped fresh ginger
- 1 small red chilli, deseeded and finely chopped
- 2 tbsp chopped fresh coriander
- 1 bay leaf
- 1 kg/2 lb 4 oz pumpkin, peeled, deseeded and diced
- 600 ml/1 pint vegetable stock
- salt and pepper
- single cream, to garnish

1 Heat the oil in a saucepan over a medium heat. Add the onion and garlic and cook, stirring, for 4 minutes, until slightly soft. Add the ginger, chilli, coriander, bay leaf and pumpkin and cook, stirring, for 3 minutes.

2 Pour in the stock and bring to the boil. Using a slotted spoon, skim any scum from the surface. Reduce the heat and simmer gently, stirring occasionally, for 25 minutes, or until the pumpkin is tender. Remove from the heat, take out and discard the bay leaf and leave to cool slightly.

3 Transfer the soup to a food processor and blend until smooth (you may have to do this in batches). Return the mixture to the saucepan and season to taste. Reheat gently, stirring. Remove from the heat, pour into four warmed soup bowls, garnish each one with a swirl of cream and serve.

Chicken Liver
PÂTÉ

Serves 4–6

- 200 g/7 oz butter
- 225 g/8 oz trimmed chicken livers, thawed if frozen
- 2 tbsp Marsala wine or brandy
- 1½ tsp chopped fresh sage
- 1 garlic clove, roughly chopped
- 150 ml/5 fl oz double cream
- salt and pepper
- fresh bay leaves or sage leaves, to garnish
- Melba toast (see Cook's note, right), to serve

Cook's note...

To make Melba toast, grill slices of white bread on both sides until golden. Cut off and discard the crusts and slice the bread in half horizontally. Grill the cut sides until golden and the edges are curling. Cool and store in an airtight container until required.

1 Melt 40 g/1½ oz of the butter in a large, heavy-based frying pan. Add the chicken livers and cook over a medium heat for 4 minutes on each side. They should be brown on the outside but still pink in the centre. Transfer to a food processor and process until finely chopped.

2 Stir the Marsala into the frying pan, scraping up any sediment with a wooden spoon, then add to the food processor with the chopped sage, garlic and 100 g/3½ oz of the remaining butter. Process until smooth. Add the cream, season to taste and process until thoroughly combined and smooth. Spoon the pâté into a dish or individual ramekins, smooth the surface and leave to cool completely.

3 Melt the remaining butter in a small saucepan, then spoon it over the surface of the pâté, leaving any sediment in the saucepan. Garnish with herb leaves, leave to cool, then cover and chill in the refrigerator. Serve with Melba toast.

Double Cheese
SOUFFLÉS

Makes 6
- 2 tbsp finely grated Parmesan cheese
- 175 ml/6 fl oz milk
- 25 g/1 oz butter, plus extra for greasing
- 25 g/1 oz self-raising flour
- whole nutmeg, for grating
- 100 g/3½ oz soft goat's cheese

Cook's note...

You can vary the types of cheeses used in these soufflés, but always choose a full-flavoured, hard cheese to complement the taste of the goat's cheese.

- 70 g/2½ oz mature Cheddar cheese, grated
- 2 large eggs, separated
- salt and pepper

1 Preheat the oven to 200°C/400°F/Gas Mark 6. Put a baking sheet in the oven to warm. Generously grease the inside of 6 small ramekins with butter, add half the Parmesan cheese and shake to coat the butter.

2 Warm the milk in a small saucepan. Melt the remaining butter in a separate saucepan over a medium heat. Add the flour, stir well to combine and cook, stirring, for 2 minutes until smooth. Add a little of the warmed milk and stir until absorbed. Continue to add the milk a little at a time, stirring constantly, until you have a rich, smooth sauce. Season to taste, and grate in a little nutmeg. Add the goat's and Cheddar cheeses to the sauce and stir until well combined and melted.

3 Remove from the heat and leave the sauce to cool a little, then add the egg yolks and stir to combine. In a separate bowl, whisk the egg whites until stiff. Fold a tablespoonful of the egg whites into the cheese sauce, then gradually fold in the remaining egg whites. Spoon into the prepared ramekins and scatter over the remaining Parmesan cheese.

4 Place the ramekins on the prepared baking sheet and bake in the preheated oven for 15 minutes until puffed up and brown. Remove from the oven and serve immediately. The soufflés will collapse quite quickly when taken from the oven, so have your serving plates ready to take the soufflés to the table.

Chestnut, Mushroom &
MADEIRA TARTS

Makes 12

Pastry
- 225 g/8 oz plain flour, plus extra for dusting
- pinch of salt
- 100 g/3½ oz unsalted butter, chilled and diced, plus extra for greasing

Filling
- 25 g/1 oz unsalted butter
- 1 tsp olive oil
- 1 shallot, finely chopped
- 1 garlic clove, crushed
- 8 cooked chestnuts, peeled and roughly chopped
- 200 g/7 oz chestnut mushrooms, chopped
- 2 tbsp Madeira
- 150 ml/5 fl oz double cream
- 1 egg, plus 1 egg yolk
- salt and pepper
- chopped fresh parsley, to garnish

1 Lightly grease a 12-hole muffin tin with butter. Sift the flour into a large bowl, add the salt and rub in the remaining butter until the mixture resembles breadcrumbs. Add a little cold water – just enough to bring the dough together. Knead the dough briefly on a floured work surface.

2 Divide the pastry in half. Roll out one piece of pastry and, using a 9-cm/3½-inch plain pastry cutter, cut out six rounds, then flatten each round with a rolling pin into a 12-cm/4½-inch round. Repeat with the other half of pastry until you have 12 rounds of pastry, then use to line the prepared muffin tin. Chill in the refrigerator for 30 minutes.

3 Meanwhile, preheat the oven to 200°C/400°F/Gas Mark 6 and make the filling. Melt the butter with the oil in a small frying pan over a low heat, add the shallot and garlic and cook, stirring occasionally, for 5–8 minutes until the shallot is transparent and soft. Add the chestnuts and mushrooms and cook, stirring, for 2 minutes, then add the Madeira and simmer for 2 minutes.

4 Line the pastry cases with baking paper and fill with baking beans, then bake in the preheated oven for 10 minutes. Carefully lift out the paper and beans, and reduce the oven temperature to 190°C/375°F/Gas Mark 5. Stir the cream, whole egg and egg yolk into the mushroom mixture and season well. Divide the mushroom mixture between the pastry cases and bake for 10 minutes. Leave to cool in the tin for 5 minutes, then carefully remove from the tin, garnish with chopped parsley and serve.

Festive Prawn
COCK TAIL

Makes 8

- 125 ml/4 fl oz tomato ketchup
- 1 tsp chilli sauce
- 1 tsp Worcestershire sauce
- 1 kg/2 lb 6 oz cooked tiger prawns
- 2 ruby grapefruits
- lettuce leaves, shredded
- 2 avocados, peeled, stoned and diced

Mayonnaise
- 2 large egg yolks
- 1 tsp English mustard powder
- 1 tsp salt
- 300 ml/10 fl oz groundnut oil
- 1 tsp white wine vinegar
- pepper

To garnish
- lime slices and fresh dill sprigs

1 To make the mayonnaise, put the egg yolks in a bowl, add the mustard powder, pepper to taste and the salt and beat together well. Pour the oil into a jug and make sure that your bowl is secure on the work surface by sitting it on a damp cloth. Using an electric or hand whisk, begin to whisk the egg yolks, adding just 1 drop of the oil. Make sure that this has been thoroughly absorbed before adding another drop and whisking well.

2 Continue adding the oil one drop at a time until the mixture thickens and stiffens – at this point, whisk in the vinegar and then continue to dribble in the remaining oil very slowly in a thin stream, whisking constantly, until you have used up all the oil and you have a thick mayonnaise.

3 Mix the mayonnaise, tomato ketchup, chilli sauce and Worcestershire sauce together in a small bowl. Cover with clingfilm and chill in the refrigerator until required. Remove the heads from the prawns and peel off the shells, leaving the tails intact. Slit along the length of the back of each prawn with a sharp knife and remove and discard the dark vein. Cut off a slice from the top and bottom of each grapefruit, then peel off the skin and all the white pith. Cut between the membranes to separate the segments.

4 Make a bed of shredded lettuce in the base of eight glass dishes. Divide the prawns, grapefruit segments and avocados between them and spoon over the mayonnaise dressing. Serve garnished with lime slices and dill sprigs.

Smoked Turkey & Stuffing
PARCELS

Makes 12

- 12 slices smoked turkey breast
- 6 tbsp cranberry sauce or jelly
- 420 g/14 oz Sage, Onion & Apple Stuffing (see page 29)
- 24 sheets filo pastry, thawed if frozen
- 70 g/2½ oz butter, melted

Cook's note...
You can add a few chopped chestnuts or other Christmas leftovers to these parcels, or replace the turkey with cooked chicken.

1 Preheat the oven to 190°C/375°F/Gas Mark 5. Put a non-stick baking sheet into the oven to heat.

2 For each parcel, spread a slice of smoked turkey with a teaspoonful of cranberry sauce, spoon 35 g/1¼ oz of the stuffing into the centre and roll up the turkey slice. Lay one sheet of filo pastry on a work surface and brush with a little of the melted butter. Put another sheet on top, then put the rolled-up turkey in the centre. Add a little more cranberry sauce, then carefully fold the filo pastry around the turkey, tucking under the ends to form a neat parcel. Repeat to make 12 parcels.

3 Place the parcels on the prepared baking sheet, brush with the remaining melted butter and bake in the preheated oven for 25 minutes until golden. Serve hot.

Piquant
CRAB BITES

Makes 50

- 100 g/3½ oz fresh white breadcrumbs
- 2 large eggs, separated
- 200 ml/7 fl oz crème fraîche
- 1 tsp English mustard powder
- 500 g/1 lb 2 oz fresh white crabmeat
- 1 tbsp chopped fresh dill
- groundnut oil, for frying
- salt and pepper
- 2 limes, quartered, to serve

1 Tip the breadcrumbs into a large bowl. In a separate bowl, whisk the egg yolks with the crème fraîche and mustard powder and add to the breadcrumbs with the crabmeat and dill. Season to taste and mix together well. Cover and chill in the refrigerator for 15 minutes.

2 In a clean bowl, whisk the egg whites until stiff. Lightly fold a tablespoonful of the egg whites into the crab mixture, then fold in the remaining egg whites.

3 Heat 2 tablespoons of oil in a non-stick frying pan over a medium–high heat. Drop in as many teaspoonfuls of the crab mixture as will fit in the frying pan without overcrowding, flatten slightly and cook for 2 minutes, or until brown and crisp. Flip over and cook for a further 1–2 minutes until the undersides are brown. Remove and drain on kitchen paper. Keep warm while you cook the remaining crab mixture, adding more oil to the frying pan if necessary.

4 Serve the crab bites warm with the lime quarters.

Blinis with
PRAWNS

Serves 6

- 350 g/12 oz plain flour
- 125 g/4½ oz buckwheat flour
- 2 tsp easy-blend dried yeast
- 600 ml/1 pint full-fat milk, warmed
- 6 eggs, separated
- 3 tbsp unsalted butter, melted
- 5 tbsp soured cream
- 50 g/1¾ oz clarified butter
- salt

Wasabi cream

- 200 ml/7 fl oz soured cream or crème fraîche
- ½ tsp wasabi paste, or to taste

To serve

- 300 g/10½ oz cooked prawns, peeled and deveined
- 50 g/1¾ oz pickled ginger, thinly sliced
- 2 tbsp fresh coriander leaves

1 Sift the flours together into a large bowl and stir in the yeast. Make a hollow in the centre and add the milk, then gradually beat in the flour until you have a smooth batter. Cover and chill in the refrigerator overnight.

2 Two hours before you need the blinis, remove the bowl from the refrigerator and leave the batter for 1 hour 20 minutes to return to room temperature. Beat in the egg yolks, melted butter and soured cream. In a separate bowl, whisk the egg whites until stiff, then gradually fold into the batter. Cover and leave to rest for 30 minutes.

3 Meanwhile, make the wasabi cream. Mix the soured cream and wasabi paste together in a small bowl until completely combined. Taste and add a little more wasabi paste, if you like it hotter. Season to taste with salt, cover and chill in the refrigerator.

4 To cook the blinis, heat a little of the clarified butter in a non-stick frying pan over a medium–high heat. When hot and sizzling, drop in 3–4 tablespoonfuls of the batter, spaced well apart, and cook until puffed up and tiny bubbles appear around the edges. Flip them over and cook for a few more minutes on the other side. Remove from the pan and keep warm while you cook the remaining batter. To serve, spoon a little of the wasabi cream on to a blini, add 1 or 2 prawns and a little ginger, then garnish with a few coriander leaves.

Hot Rum
PUNCH

Serves 4.3 litres/7½ pints
- 850 ml/1½ pints rum
- 850 ml/1½ pints brandy
- 600 ml/1 pint freshly
  squeezed lemon juice
- 3–4 tbsp caster sugar
- 2 litres/3½ pints boiling
  water
- slices of fruit, to decorate

Cook's note...
This warming drink is a great way to greet guests at a Christmas get-together or a much-deserved reward for those who venture out for a brisk walk on Boxing Day. Father Christmas probably deserves a glass too!

1 Mix together the rum, brandy, lemon juice and 3 tablespoons of the sugar in a punch bowl or large heatproof mixing bowl. Pour in the boiling water and stir well to mix.

2 Taste and add more sugar if required. Decorate with the fruit slices and serve immediately in heatproof glasses with handles.

Mulled Ale &
MULLED WINE

....

Makes 2.8 litres/5 pints
Mulled Ale

- 2.5 litres/4½ pints strong ale
- 300 ml/10 fl oz brandy
- 2 tbsp caster sugar
- large pinch of ground cloves
- large pinch of ground ginger

Makes 3.3 litres/5¾ pints
Mulled Wine

- 5 oranges
- 50 cloves
- thinly pared rind and juice of 4 lemons
- 850 ml/1½ pints water
- 115 g/4 oz caster sugar
- 2 cinnamon sticks
- 2 litres/3½ pints red wine
- 150 ml/5 fl oz brandy

1 For the mulled ale, put all the ingredients in a heavy-based saucepan and heat gently, stirring, until the sugar has dissolved. Continue to heat so that it is simmering but not boiling. Remove the saucepan from the heat and serve the ale immediately in heatproof glasses.

2 For the mulled wine, prick the skins of three of the oranges all over with a fork and stud with the cloves, then set aside. Thinly pare the rind and squeeze the juice from the remaining oranges.

3 Put the orange rind and juice, lemon rind and juice, water, sugar and cinnamon in a heavy-based saucepan and bring to the boil over a medium heat, stirring occasionally, until the sugar has dissolved. Boil for 2 minutes without stirring, then remove from the heat, stir once and leave to stand for 10 minutes. Strain the liquid into a heatproof jug, pressing down on the contents of the sieve to extract all the juice.

4 Pour the wine into a separate saucepan and add the strained spiced juices, the brandy and the clove-studded oranges. Simmer gently without boiling, then remove the saucepan from the heat. Strain into heatproof glasses and serve hot.

Cinnamon
APPLE CUP

Makes 3.7 litres/6½ pints

- 40 cloves
- 2 apples, cored, quartered and thickly sliced
- 2 oranges, quartered and thickly sliced
- 4 cinnamon sticks
- 1.8 litres/3 pints pressed apple juice
- 600 ml/1 pint orange juice
- 600 ml/1 pint dark rum (optional)

1 Insert one clove into each apple slice and place in a large saucepan with the orange pieces, cinnamon sticks, apple juice and orange juice.

2 Place over a low heat and simmer for 20 minutes to allow the flavours to infuse.

3 Remove the pan from the heat. Add rum, if using, and serve warm, ladled into heatproof glasses.

3

The

MAIN EVENT

At The Christmas Dinner
TABLE

I t's a sad fact that most of us don't have a troupe of pointy-eared little helpers to lend a hand with preparing the Christmas dinner – and unfortunately it can also be true that sometimes what help we do have can be more of a hindrance! Preparing a Christmas dinner is a lot of work – there's no point in pretending otherwise – but it's work that, if done properly, should pay dividends. And Christmas is a time for giving, after all!

There are few more appetising sights than a well-laid Christmas dinner table. Lush, overflowing, sparkling, steaming… it should put one in mind of a medieval banquet: a sumptuous feast for all the senses, a riot of colour and texture and smell and promised taste. Which should be simple to achieve, right?

Well – yes, actually. So long as you plan properly, there's no reason why your table shouldn't look spectacular. A well-thought-out seating plan helps of course, with guests requiring special dietary requirements sat appropriately (putting a vegan next to the turkey carver, for example, is probably not a great idea).

Work out exactly where you intend to place each bowl, bottle, tureen and serving plate so that everyone can help themselves to something without having to wait too long – and for an effective, attractive way to really make your table stand out, fill in the spaces with bunches of fresh holly and ivy.

And of course, one shouldn't forget the Christmas wreath! Think of your dinner table decorations beginning the moment your guests knock on your front door – and what better way to set the scene than with a beautiful, natural door wreath? For this project, you will need a tape measure, scissors, strong double-sided tape, floristry wire and long-nosed pliers.

Christmas Door Wreath

Materials

- plain deep-red fabric, red gingham and ruby raw-silk fabric, each 2.5 cm x 1.5 metres/1 inch x 59 inches
- polystyrene wreath 24 cm/9½ inches in diameter
- red gingham 2.5 cm x 50 cm/1 x 20 inches
- 21 holly leaves, 16 about 6 cm/2½ inches and 5 about 4 cm/1½ inches in length
- 2 fir cones on wire about 5 cm/2 inches
- fake berries on flexible stems
- craft equipment (see bottom of page 64)

1 Wrap the red fabric strip around the wreath – the point at which you start and finish will become the bottom of the wreath. Use double-sided tape to secure the ends. Do not worry about covering all the polystyrene at this stage.

2 Repeat with the larger length of gingham, starting and ending in the same place and focusing on covering more of the polystyrene. Repeat with the raw silk to cover the remaining polystyrene.

3 Wrap the smaller piece of gingham over where the other strips started and ended as many times as possible, tying the ends in a tight knot. Trim the ends. Use the scissors to trim any stray threads.

4 Thread all the holly leaves with the floristry wire, using the pliers to help direct the wire into the main veins of the holly. The smaller leaves should be together. Use the pliers to pierce all around the polystyrene wreath and insert the large holly leaves into the holes. The smaller leaves should be by the wrapped gingham.

5 Gently push the fir cones under the wrapped gingham with the berries, and finish with the smaller wired holly in between. Push a length of wire into the back of the wreath to make a loop to hang the wreath.

Prime Rib of
BEEF AU JUS

Serves 8

- 2.7 kg/6 lb rib of beef
- 55 g/2 oz butter, softened
- 1½ tsp sea salt flakes
- 1 tbsp ground black pepper
- 2 tbsp flour
- 1 litre/1¾ pints beef stock
- roast potatoes and
  vegetables, to serve

1 Remove the rib of beef from the fridge and place bone-side down in a
deep-sided roasting tin. Rub the entire surface of the meat with butter,
and coat evenly with the salt and black pepper.

2 Leave the beef to reach room temperature for 1 hour. Preheat the oven to
230°C/450°F/Gas Mark 8. Place the meat in the preheated oven and allow to
roast uncovered for 20 minutes to sear the outside of the roast.

3 Reduce the heat to 165°C/325°F/Gas Mark 3 and roast for 15 minutes per
450 g/1 lb of meat for medium-rare (plus or minus 15 minutes for well done
and rare respectively). Transfer the meat to a large platter and cover with foil.
Allow to rest for 30 minutes before serving.

4 Meanwhile, pour off all but 2 tablespoons of the fat from the tin and place the
roasting tin over a medium heat. Add the flour to the roasting tin and simmer,
stirring with a wooden spoon for 1 minute to form a thick paste. Pour in a
ladleful of beef stock and allow to boil, then beat into the paste, scraping all
the caramelized beef drippings from the bottom of the tin until smooth. Repeat
with the remaining stock, a ladleful at a time.

5 Simmer for 10 minutes to reduce and thicken slightly. Season to taste then
strain the sauce and keep warm.

6 Cut the beef free from its bone and carve thinly. Serve the 'jus' alongside the
carved beef, accompanied by vegetables and roast potatoes.

Glazed
GAMMON

Serves 8

- a 4-kg/8¾-lb gammon joint
- 1 apple, cored and chopped
- 1 onion, chopped
- 300 ml/10 fl oz dry cider
- 6 black peppercorns
- 1 bouquet garni
- 1 bay leaf
- about 50 cloves
- 4 tbsp demerara sugar

Cook's note...

You can buy ready-made bouquet garni in little sachets like teabags. However, fresh herbs are much more flavoursome. Tie together 2–3 fresh parsley sprigs, 1 fresh thyme sprig and a fresh bay leaf into a bundle. For extra flavour, tie them together with a strip of celery rather than string.

1 Put the gammon in a large saucepan and add enough cold water to cover. Bring to the boil and skim off the scum that rises to the surface. Reduce the heat and simmer for 30 minutes. Drain the gammon and return to the saucepan. Add the apple, onion, cider, peppercorns, bouquet garni, bay leaf and a few of the cloves. Pour in enough fresh water to cover and return to the boil. Reduce the heat, cover and simmer for 3 hours 20 minutes.

2 Preheat the oven to 200°C/400°F/Gas Mark 6. Take the saucepan off the heat and set aside to cool slightly. Remove the gammon from the cooking liquid and, while it is still warm, loosen the rind with a sharp knife, then peel it off and discard. Score the fat into diamond shapes and stud with the remaining cloves.

3 Place the gammon on a rack in a roasting tin and sprinkle with the sugar. Roast in the preheated oven, basting occasionally with the cooking liquid, for 20 minutes. Serve hot, or cold later.

Traditional Roast
CHICKEN

Serves 6

- a 2.25-kg/5-lb free-range chicken
- 55 g/2 oz butter
- 2 tbsp chopped fresh lemon thyme
- 1 lemon, quartered
- 125 ml/4 fl oz white wine
- salt and pepper
- 6 fresh thyme sprigs, to garnish
- two potato mash, to serve (see page 88)

Cook's note...

You can stuff your chicken with a traditional stuffing, such as sage and onion, or with fruit like apricots and prunes, but often the best way is to keep it simple. If you do stuff the chicken, remember to stuff just the neck end or the bird might not cook through.

1 Preheat the oven to 220°C/425°F/Gas Mark 7. Make sure the chicken is clean, wiping it inside and out with kitchen paper, and place in a roasting tin. In a bowl, soften the butter with a fork, mix in the thyme and season well to taste. Butter the chicken all over with the herb butter, inside and out, and place the lemon quarters inside the body cavity. Pour the wine over the chicken.

2 Roast in the centre of the preheated oven for 20 minutes. Reduce the temperature to 190°C/375°F/Gas Mark 5 and roast for a further 1¼ hours, basting frequently. Cover with foil if the skin begins to brown too much. If the tin dries out, add a little more wine or water.

3 Test that the chicken is cooked by piercing the thickest part of the leg with a sharp knife or skewer and making sure the juices run clear. Remove from the oven. Transfer the chicken to a warmed serving plate, cover loosely with foil and leave to rest for 10 minutes before carving. Place the roasting tin on the top of the stove and bubble the pan juices gently over a low heat until they have reduced and are thick and glossy. Season to taste. Serve the chicken with the pan juices and two potato mash. Garnish with the thyme sprigs.

Yuletide
GOOSE

Serves 4–6
- a 3.5–4.5-kg/7¾–10-lb oven-ready goose
- 1 tsp salt
- 4 pears
- 1 tbsp lemon juice
- 4 tbsp butter
- 2 tbsp honey

Cook's note...
'Christmas is coming and the goose is getting fat' – and they do look like extremely big birds. However, there is proportionately a lot less meat on a goose than on a turkey or chicken because a goose's rib cage is so large.

1 Preheat the oven to 220°C/425°F/Gas Mark 7. Rinse the goose and pat dry. Use a fork to prick the skin all over, then rub with the salt. Place the bird upside down on a rack in a roasting tin. Roast in the preheated oven for 30 minutes. Drain off the fat. Turn the bird over and roast for 15 minutes. Drain off the fat.

2 Reduce the heat to 180°C/350°F/Gas Mark 4 and roast for 15 minutes per 450 g/1 lb. Cover with foil 15 minutes before the end of the cooking time. Check that the bird is cooked by inserting a knife between the legs and body. If the juices run clear, it is ready. Remove from the oven. Transfer the goose to a warmed serving platter, cover loosely with foil and leave to rest.

3 Peel and halve the pears, then brush with the lemon juice. Melt the butter and honey in a saucepan over a low heat, then add the pears. Cook, stirring, for 5–10 minutes until tender. Remove from the heat, arrange the pears around the goose and pour the sweet juices over the bird, then serve.

Madeira &
BLUEBERRY DUCK

Serves 4

- 4 duck breasts (skin left on)
- 4 garlic cloves, chopped
- grated rind and juice of 1 orange
- 1 tbsp chopped fresh parsley
- salt and pepper

Madeira & blueberry sauce

- 150 g/5½ oz blueberries
- 250 ml/9 fl oz Madeira
- 1 tbsp redcurrant jelly

To serve

- new potatoes
- selection of green vegetables

1 Use a sharp knife to make several shallow diagonal cuts in each duck breast. Put the duck in a glass bowl with the garlic, orange rind and juice, and the parsley. Season to taste and stir well. Turn the duck in the mixture until thoroughly coated. Cover the bowl with clingfilm and leave in the refrigerator to marinate for at least 1 hour.

2 Heat a dry, non-stick frying pan over a medium heat. Add the duck breasts and cook for 4 minutes, then turn them over and cook for a further 4 minutes, or according to taste. Remove from the heat, cover the frying pan and leave to stand for 5 minutes.

3 Halfway through the cooking time, put the blueberries, Madeira and redcurrant jelly into a separate saucepan. Bring to the boil. Reduce the heat and simmer for 10 minutes, then remove from the heat.

4 Slice the duck breasts and transfer to warmed serving plates. Serve with the sauce poured over and accompanied by new potatoes and a selection of green vegetables.

Roast
PHEASANT

Serves 4
- 100 g/3½ oz butter, slightly softened
- 1 tbsp chopped fresh thyme
- 1 tbsp chopped fresh parsley
- 2 oven-ready young pheasants
- 4 tbsp vegetable oil
- 125 ml/4 fl oz red wine
- salt and pepper

Game chips
- 650 g/1 lb 7oz potatoes
- sunflower oil, for frying

1 Preheat the oven to 190°C/375°F/Gas Mark 5. Put the butter in a small bowl and mix in the chopped herbs. Lift the skins off the pheasants, taking care not to tear them, and push the herb butter under the skins. Season to taste.

2 Pour the oil into a roasting tin, add the pheasants and roast in the preheated oven for 45 minutes, basting occasionally. Remove from the oven, pour over the wine, then return to the oven and cook for a further 15 minutes, or until cooked through. Check that each bird is cooked by inserting a knife between the legs and body. If the juices run clear, they are cooked.

3 To make the game chips, peel the potatoes and cut into wafer-thin slices. Immediately place in a bowl of cold water. Heat the oil in a deep fryer to 190°C/375°F, or until a cube of bread browns in 30 seconds. Drain the potato slices and pat dry with kitchen paper. Deep-fry, in batches, for 2–3 minutes, stirring to keep them from sticking, and remove with a slotted spoon. Drain on kitchen paper.

4 Remove the pheasants from the oven, cover loosely with foil and leave to rest for 15 minutes. Serve on a warmed serving platter surrounded with game chips.

Festive Beef
WELLINGTON

Serves 4

- 750 g/1 lb 10 oz thick beef fillet
- 2 tbsp butter
- 2 tbsp vegetable oil
- 1 garlic clove, chopped
- 1 onion, chopped
- 175 g/6 oz chestnut mushrooms, thinly sliced
- 1 tbsp chopped fresh sage
- 350 g/12 oz puff pastry, thawed if frozen
- 1 egg, beaten
- salt and pepper

1 Preheat the oven to 220°C/425°F/Gas Mark 7. Put the beef in a roasting tin, spread with the butter and season to taste. Roast in the preheated oven for 30 minutes, then remove from the oven.

2 Meanwhile, heat the oil in a saucepan over a medium heat. Add the garlic and onion and cook, stirring, for 3 minutes. Stir in salt and pepper to taste, the mushrooms and the sage and cook, stirring frequently, for 5 minutes. Remove from the heat.

3 Roll out the pastry into a rectangle large enough to enclose the beef, then place the beef in the centre and spread the mushroom mixture over it. Bring the long sides of the pastry together over the beef and seal with beaten egg. Tuck the short ends over (trim away excess pastry) and seal. Place on a baking sheet, seam-side down. Make two slits in the top. Decorate with dough shapes and brush with egg. Bake in the preheated oven for 40 minutes. Remove from the oven, cut into thick slices and serve.

Herbed
SALMON

Serves 4

- 4 salmon fillets, about 175 g/6 oz each, skin removed
- 2 tbsp olive oil
- 1 tbsp chopped fresh dill
- 1 tbsp snipped fresh chives, plus extra to garnish
- salt and pepper

Hollandaise sauce

- 3 egg yolks
- 1 tbsp water
- 225 g/8 oz butter, cut into small cubes
- juice of 1 lemon
- salt and pepper

To serve

- freshly cooked sprouting broccoli
- sesame seeds

1 Preheat the grill to medium. Rinse the fish fillets under cold running water and pat dry with kitchen paper. Season to taste. Combine the oil with the dill and chives in a bowl, then brush the mixture over the fish. Transfer to the grill and cook for 6–8 minutes, turning once and brushing with more oil and herb mixture, until cooked to your taste.

2 Meanwhile, make the sauce. Put the egg yolks in a heatproof bowl over a saucepan of gently simmering water (or use a double boiler). Add the water and season to taste. Reduce the heat until the water in the saucepan is barely simmering and whisk constantly until the mixture begins to thicken. Whisk in the butter, one piece at a time, until the mixture is thick and shiny. Whisk in the lemon juice, then remove from the heat.

3 Remove the salmon from the grill and transfer to warmed individual serving plates. Pour the sauce over the fish and garnish with snipped fresh chives. Serve immediately on a bed of sprouting broccoli, garnished with sesame seeds.

Wild Mushroom
FILO PARCELS

Serves 6

- 30 g/1 oz dried porcini mushrooms
- 70 g/2½ oz butter
- 1 shallot, finely chopped
- 1 garlic clove, crushed
- 100 g/3½ oz chestnut mushrooms, sliced
- 100 g/3½ oz white cap mushrooms, sliced
- 200 g/7 oz wild mushrooms, chopped
- 150 g/5½ oz basmati rice, cooked and cooled
- 2 tbsp dry sherry
- 1 tbsp soy sauce or mushroom sauce
- 1 tbsp chopped fresh flat-leaf parsley
- 18 sheets filo pastry, thawed if frozen
- vegetable oil, for oiling
- 350 ml/12 fl oz crème fraîche
- 50 ml/2 fl oz Madeira
- salt and pepper

1 Put the dried mushrooms in a heatproof bowl and just cover with boiling water. Leave to soak for 20 minutes. Meanwhile, melt half the butter in a large frying pan over a low heat, add the shallot and garlic and cook, stirring occasionally, for 5–8 minutes until the shallot is transparent and soft. Add all the fresh mushrooms and cook, stirring, for 2–3 minutes.

2 Preheat the oven to 200°C/400°F/Gas Mark 6. Drain the dried mushrooms, reserving the soaking liquid, roughly chop and add to the frying pan with the rice, sherry, soy sauce and parsley. Season well, mix together and simmer until most of the liquid has evaporated.

3 Melt the remaining butter in a small saucepan. Lay one sheet of filo pastry on a work surface and brush with melted butter. Put another sheet on top and brush with butter, then top with a third sheet. Spoon some of the mushroom mixture into the centre, then fold in the edges to form a parcel. Use a little more of the melted butter to make sure that the edges are secure. Repeat to make six parcels.

4 Place the parcels on a lightly oiled baking sheet and brush with the remaining melted butter. Bake in the preheated oven for 25–30 minutes until golden.

5 Meanwhile, to make the sauce, heat the reserved soaking liquid in a saucepan, add the crème fraîche and Madeira and stir over a low heat until heated through. Season to taste and serve with the parcels.

Mixed Nut
ROAST

Serves 4

- 2 tbsp butter, plus extra for greasing
- 2 garlic cloves, chopped
- 1 large onion, chopped
- 50 g/1¾ oz pine kernels, toasted
- 75 g/2¾ oz hazelnuts, toasted
- 50 g/1¾ oz walnuts, ground
- 50 g/1¾ oz cashew nuts, ground
- 100 g/3½ oz fresh wholemeal breadcrumbs
- 1 egg, lightly beaten
- 2 tbsp chopped fresh thyme

- 250 ml/9 fl oz vegetable stock
- salt and pepper
- fresh thyme sprigs, to garnish
- cranberry sauce, to serve (see page 32)
- Brussels sprouts, to serve

Cook's note...

Nuts contain a lot of oil and will turn rancid if they are stored too long. Buy them in small quantities, store in airtight containers and keep an eye on the 'use by' dates. It is probably worth buying fresh nuts for this festive treat.

1 Preheat the oven to 180°C/350°F/Gas Mark 4. Grease a loaf tin with butter and line it with greaseproof paper. Melt the remaining butter in a saucepan over a medium heat. Add the garlic and onion and cook, stirring, for 5 minutes, until softened. Remove from the heat. Grind the pine kernels and hazelnuts. Stir all the nuts into the saucepan, add the breadcrumbs, egg, thyme and stock and season to taste.

2 Spoon the mixture into the loaf tin and level the surface. Cook in the preheated oven for 30 minutes, or until cooked through and golden. The loaf is cooked when a skewer inserted into the centre comes out clean.

3 Remove the nut roast from the oven and turn out onto a warmed serving dish. Garnish with thyme sprigs and serve with cranberry sauce and Brussels sprouts.

Buttered Chestnut Brussels
SPROUTS

Serves 4

- 350 g/12 oz Brussels sprouts, trimmed
- 3 tbsp butter
- 100 g/3½ oz canned whole chestnuts
- pinch of grated nutmeg
- salt and pepper
- 50 g/1¾ oz flaked almonds, to garnish

1 Bring a large saucepan of salted water to the boil. Add the Brussels sprouts and cook for 5 minutes. Drain thoroughly.

2 Melt the butter in a large saucepan over a medium heat. Add the Brussels sprouts and cook, stirring, for 3 minutes, then add the chestnuts and nutmeg. Season to taste and stir well.

3 Cook for a further 2 minutes, stirring, then remove from the heat. Transfer to a warmed serving dish, garnish with almonds and serve.

Two Potato
MASH

Serves 6

- 2 large orange sweet potatoes
- ½ tsp vegetable oil
- 4 potatoes
- 25 g/1 oz butter
- 125 ml/4 fl oz double cream
- whole nutmeg, for grating
- salt and pepper

Cook's note...

If you make the mash in advance, it can be put in a greased gratin dish, dotted with a little extra butter and cooked under the grill until golden on top.

1 Preheat the oven to 190°C/375°F/Gas Mark 5. Rub the sweet potatoes with the oil, then bake in the preheated oven for 20–25 minutes until tender.

2 Meanwhile, peel the potatoes, then cook in a large saucepan of boiling water until tender. Drain well and put in a colander. Cover with a clean tea towel to absorb the steam and leave to stand until cooled. Mash the potatoes or pass through a potato ricer.

3 Scoop out the flesh from the sweet potatoes and mix well with the potato in a warmed bowl. Discard the sweet potato skins. Melt the butter with the cream in a small saucepan, then pour half over the potato mixture and beat well with a wooden spoon. Add the remaining cream mixture a little at a time until you achieve the consistency you like. Season to taste, and add a grating of nutmeg. Beat again, then serve.

Spiced Winter
VEGETABLES

Serves 4

- 4 parsnips, scrubbed and trimmed but left unpeeled
- 4 carrots, scrubbed and trimmed but left unpeeled
- 2 onions, quartered
- 1 red onion, quartered
- 3 leeks, trimmed and cut into 6-cm/2½-inch slices
- 6 garlic cloves, left unpeeled and whole
- 6 tbsp extra virgin olive oil
- ½ tsp mild chilli powder
- pinch of paprika
- salt and pepper

Cook's note...

Providing there is room in the oven, these vegetables are ideal for Christmas lunch, because they offer a selection of different flavours without taking up the entire hob and several saucepans.

1 Preheat the oven to 220°C/425°F/Gas Mark 7. Bring a large saucepan of water to the boil.

2 Cut the parsnips and carrots into wedges of similar size. Add them to the saucepan and cook for 5 minutes. Drain thoroughly and place in an ovenproof dish with the onions, leeks and garlic. Pour over the oil, sprinkle in the spices and season to taste, then mix until all the vegetables are well coated.

3 Roast in the preheated oven for at least 1 hour. Turn the vegetables from time to time until they are tender and starting to colour. Remove from the oven, transfer to a warmed serving dish and serve immediately.

Honey-glazed
RED CABBAGE

Serves 4

- 2 tbsp butter
- 1 garlic clove, chopped
- 650 g/1 lb 7 oz red cabbage, shredded
- 150 g/5½ oz sultanas
- 1 tbsp clear honey
- 100 ml/3½ fl oz red wine
- 100 ml/3½ fl oz water

Cook's note...
Red cabbage is a classic accompaniment to game, such as pheasant, and roast pork or gammon. It also goes well with some poultry, notably goose and duck, counteracting the richness of the meat.

1 Melt the butter in a large saucepan over a medium heat. Add the garlic and cook, stirring, for 1 minute, until slightly soft.

2 Add the cabbage and sultanas, then stir in the honey. Cook for 1 minute more. Pour in the wine and water and bring to the boil. Reduce the heat, cover and simmer gently, stirring occasionally, for 45 minutes, or until the cabbage is cooked. Serve hot.

Chestnut & Sausage
STUFFING

Serves 6–8
- 225 g/8 oz pork sausage meat
- 225 g/8 oz unsweetened chestnut purée
- 85 g/3 oz walnuts, chopped
- 115 g/4 oz dried apricots, chopped
- 2 tbsp chopped fresh parsley
- 2 tbsp snipped fresh chives
- 2 tsp chopped fresh sage
- 4–5 tbsp double cream
- salt and pepper

1 Combine the sausage meat and chestnut purée in a bowl, then stir in the walnuts, apricots, parsley, chives and sage. Stir in enough cream to make a firm, but not dry, mixture. Season to taste.

2 If you are planning to stuff a turkey or goose, fill the neck cavity only to ensure the bird cooks all the way through. It is safer and more reliable to cook the stuffing separately, either rolled into small balls and placed on a baking sheet or spooned into an ovenproof dish.

3 Cook the separate stuffing in a preheated oven for 30–40 minutes at 190°C/375°F/Gas Mark 5. It should be allowed a longer time to cook if you are roasting a bird at a lower temperature in the same oven.

Pork, Cranberry &
HERB STUFFING

Serves 6

- 1 tbsp vegetable oil, plus extra for oiling
- 1 onion, finely chopped
- 2 celery sticks, chopped
- 450 g/1 lb pork sausage meat
- 50 g/1¾ oz fresh white or wholemeal breadcrumbs
- 50 g/1¾ oz dried cranberries
- 70 g/2½ oz fresh cranberries
- 1 tbsp chopped fresh parsley

- 1 tbsp chopped fresh sage
- 1 tbsp chopped fresh thyme leaves
- 1 large egg, beaten
- salt and pepper

Cook's note...
This stuffing can be made in advance and frozen, as long as the sausage meat has not previously been frozen. Thaw the stuffing thoroughly before cooking.

1 Heat the oil in a heavy-based frying pan over a medium heat, add the onion and celery and cook, stirring frequently, for 10 minutes until the onion is transparent and soft.

2 Meanwhile, preheat the oven to 190°C/375°F/Gas Mark 5. Break up the sausage meat in a large bowl. Add the breadcrumbs, dried and fresh cranberries and the herbs and mix together well. Add the cooked onion and celery, then the egg. Season well and mix together thoroughly.

3 Form the stuffing into balls, place on an oiled baking sheet and bake in the preheated oven for 25 minutes. Alternatively, spoon into two foil tins, level the surface and bake for 45 minutes.

Christmas
SALAD

....

Serves 4

- 125 ml/4 fl oz olive oil
- 4 tbsp lemon juice
- 3 tbsp cranberry sauce
- 1 tbsp grainy mustard
- 280 g/10 oz left-over cooked vegetables (such as carrots, green beans, broccoli)
- 225 g/8 oz left-over roast potatoes
- 300 g/10½ oz rocket or watercress
- 500 g/1 lb 2 oz cooked turkey, sliced
- 55 g/2 oz fresh Parmesan shavings

1 Make the salad dressing by whisking the olive oil, lemon juice, cranberry sauce and mustard together with a fork until combined.

2 Chop the left-over vegetables and potatoes into bite-sized pieces and toss, together with half the dressing, in a large bowl.

3 Divide the rocket or watercress between four serving plates. Pile the vegetables on top and arrange the turkey over the vegetables. Scatter the Parmesan shavings over the top and serve with the remaining dressing, according to taste.

4

Desserts &

CAKES

And Now For Something
SWEET...

Christmas treats need not come pre-wrapped from the shops. Just as those 'presentation pack' stockings filled with chocolate bars are a pretty sad substitute for the thrill of a home-made stocking stuffed with goodies, so preparing your own Yuletide treats makes for an immensely more rewarding experience.

And if eating them is nice – and of course it is! – then making them can also be fun. The beauty of all those desserts and cakes is that most of them can be made in advance... making the run-up to Christmas that little bit longer as well as providing an early excuse to get stuck in. Nothing signals the start of Christmas more than getting together the ingredients for the Christmas cake or pudding. It suddenly hits you – Christmas really is coming!

Don't restrict yourself to the traditional treats. Yes, of course you'll want a panettone – and brandy snaps – but there's no reason to stop there; and there's also no reason to limit your sweet fancies to the big day itself. Who says a Yule log can't be enjoyed a week before Christmas? Who says mince pies and brandy butter have to be saved for those drinks-and-nibbles parties? Indulge yourself, fill your home with the delicious aroma of fresh baking... and start on the seasonal sweet things at the earliest decent opportunity!

While you're in the mood for making something fun, creating a gingerbread house is a lovely way to set the festive tone – and a great way to involve the children in the celebrations. Or if you would like to create something for the home, why not make our festive reindeer tea-light box? For this project, you will need scissors, masking tape, craft knife, steel-edged ruler, cutting mat, bone folder or scoring tool and strong double-sided tape.

Reindeer
Tea-light Box

Materials

- 300 gsm Bockingford (slightly textured) paper
- thick tracing paper
- board 2 mm/¹⁄₁₆ inch thick
- clear glass tea-light holders
- tea lights
- craft materials (see bottom of page 102)

1 Enlarge the box templates on page 221 on a photocopier as directed and cut out using scissors. You may need to make the template in two halves.

2 Place the light box template over the Bockingford paper on a cutting mat and secure both with masking tape. Using the craft knife, cut out as many of the reindeer shapes as you want, depending on how many sides will be visible.

3 Cut out the light box, marking the position of the folds by piercing through to the paper at each end of the fold lines as you cut around. Remove the template. Align the ruler with the puncture marks and score along the lines with a bone folder or scoring tool.

4 Cut the tracing paper to the size of the panels from which you have cut motifs. Secure to the panels with double-sided tape along the top and bottom edges.

5 Construct the box, using double-sided tape to adhere the hem inside at the top of the box, for extra rigidity, and the side seam. Fold up the bottom of the box – it should look like the back of an envelope – using a few strips of double-sided tape in different directions to secure it.

6 Using the rectangular template, cut the platform from the board, then slot into the base of the light box. Place the tea lights in clear glass tea-light holders no less than 6 cm/2½ inches high and position centrally within the box. Use no more than two tea lights per box and make sure you do not leave the tea-light box unattended.

103

Traditional
APPLE PIE

Serves 8

Pastry
- 350 g/12 oz plain flour
- pinch of salt
- 85 g/3 oz butter or margarine, chilled and diced
- 85 g/3 oz lard or white vegetable fat, chilled and diced
- about 6 tbsp cold water
- beaten egg or milk, for glazing

Filling
- 750 g–1 kg/1 lb 10 oz–2 lb 4 oz cooking apples, peeled, cored and sliced
- 125 g/4½ oz soft light brown sugar or caster sugar, plus extra for sprinkling
- ½–1 tsp ground cinnamon, mixed spice or ground ginger
- 1–2 tbsp water (optional)

1 To make the pastry, sift the flour and salt into a bowl. Add the butter and fat and rub in until the mixture resembles fine breadcrumbs. Add the water and gather the mixture together into a dough. Wrap the dough in clingfilm and chill in the refrigerator for 30 minutes.

2 Preheat the oven to 220°C/425°F/Gas Mark 7. Roll out almost two thirds of the pastry thinly and use to line a deep 23-cm/9-inch pie plate or pie tin.

3 To make the filling, mix the apples with the sugar and spice and pack into the pastry case; the filling can come up above the rim. Add the water if needed, particularly if the apples are not very juicy.

4 Roll out the remaining pastry to form a lid. Dampen the edges of the pie rim with water and position the lid, pressing the edges firmly together. Trim and crimp the edges. Use the trimmings to cut out leaves or other shapes to decorate the top of the pie, dampen with water and attach. Glaze the top of the pie with beaten egg or milk, make one or two slits in the top and place the pie on a baking sheet.

5 Bake in the preheated oven for 20 minutes, then reduce the temperature to 180°C/350°F/Gas Mark 4 and bake for a further 30 minutes, or until the pastry is a light golden brown. Serve hot or cold, sprinkled with sugar.

Christmas Spiced
LOAF

**Serves 6

- 450 g/1 lb strong white flour, plus extra for dusting
- pinch of salt
- 2 tsp mixed spice
- 115 g/4 oz unsalted butter, chilled and diced
- 7-g/⅙-oz easy-blend dried yeast
- 115 g/4 oz unrefined caster sugar
- 115 g/4 oz currants
- 115 g/4 oz raisins
- 50 g/1¾ oz mixed peel, chopped
- finely grated rind of 1 orange
- 1 egg, beaten
- 150 ml/5 fl oz milk, warmed
- vegetable oil, for oiling

1 Sift the flour, salt and mixed spice into a bowl and rub in the butter until the mixture resembles breadcrumbs. Stir in the yeast, sugar, dried fruit, mixed peel and orange rind, then add the egg and the warm milk and bring together to form a soft dough.

2 Knead the dough briefly on a floured work surface. Flour a clean bowl and add the dough. Cover the bowl and leave to rise in a warm place for 2 hours.

3 Preheat the oven to 180°C/350°F/Gas Mark 4 and oil a 900-g/2-lb loaf tin. Knead the dough again briefly, then place it in the prepared tin, cover and leave to prove for 20 minutes. Bake in the preheated oven for 1 hour 10 minutes – the loaf should be golden and well risen. Leave to cool in the tin.

Dark Chocolate
YULE LOG

Serves 8

- butter, for greasing
- 150 g/5½ oz caster sugar, plus extra for sprinkling
- 4 eggs, separated
- 1 tsp almond extract
- 115 g/4 oz self-raising flour, plus extra for dusting
- 280 g/10 oz plain chocolate, broken into squares
- 225 ml/8 fl oz double cream
- 2 tbsp rum
- holly, to decorate
- icing sugar, for dusting

1 Preheat the oven to 190°C/375°F/Gas Mark 5. Grease and line a 40 x 28-cm/ 16 x 11-inch Swiss roll tin, then dust with flour.

2 Reserve 2 tablespoons of the caster sugar and whisk the remainder with the egg yolks in a bowl until thick and pale. Stir in the almond extract. Whisk the egg whites in a separate, clean bowl until soft peaks form. Gradually whisk in the reserved sugar until stiff and glossy. Sift half the flour over the egg yolk mixture and fold in, then fold in one quarter of the egg whites. Sift and fold in the remaining flour, followed by the remaining egg whites. Spoon the mixture into the prepared tin, spreading it out evenly with a palette knife. Bake in the preheated oven for 15 minutes, until lightly golden.

3 Sprinkle caster sugar over a sheet of greaseproof paper and turn out the cake on to the paper. Roll up and leave to cool.

4 Place the chocolate in a heatproof bowl. Bring the cream to boiling point in a small saucepan, then pour it over the chocolate and stir until the chocolate has melted. Beat with an electric mixer until smooth and thick. Reserve about one third of the chocolate mixture and stir the rum into the remainder. Unroll the cake and spread the chocolate and rum mixture over. Re-roll and place on a plate or silver board. Spread the reserved chocolate mixture evenly over the top and sides. Mark with a fork so that the surface resembles tree bark. Just before serving, decorate with holly and a sprinkling of icing sugar to resemble snow.

Poached
PEARS

Serves 6

- 6 Comice or other dessert pears, peeled but left whole with stalks attached
- 500 ml/18 fl oz Marsala
- 125 ml/4 fl oz water
- 1 tbsp soft brown sugar
- 1 piece of lemon rind or mandarin rind
- 1 vanilla pod
- 350 ml/12 fl oz double cream
- 1 tbsp icing sugar

Cook's note...
You can add a few pieces of chopped stem ginger to the syrup when cool and serve the pears with some stem ginger or cinnamon ice cream.

1 Put the pears in a large saucepan with the Marsala, water, brown sugar and lemon rind and bring gently to the boil, stirring to make sure that the sugar has dissolved. Reduce the heat, cover and simmer for 30 minutes until the pears are tender. Leave the pears to cool in the liquid. Remove the pears from the liquid, cover and chill in the refrigerator.

2 Discard the lemon rind and simmer the liquid for 15–20 minutes, or until syrupy. Leave to cool.

3 Cut a thin sliver of flesh from the base of each pear so that they will stand upright. Slit the vanilla pod open and scrape out the seeds into a bowl. Whisk the cream, vanilla seeds and icing sugar together in a bowl until thick. Put each pear on a dessert plate and pour over a little syrup. Serve with the vanilla cream.

Gingered Brandy
SNAPS

Makes 36

- vegetable oil, for greasing
- 115 g/4 oz unsalted butter
- 140 g/5 oz golden syrup
- 115 g/4 oz demerara sugar
- 115 g/4 oz plain flour
- 2 tsp ground ginger
- 600 ml/1 pint stiffly whipped
  double cream, to serve

1 Preheat the oven to 160°C/325°F/Gas Mark 3. Brush a non-stick baking sheet with oil. Place the butter, syrup and sugar in a saucepan and set over a low heat, stirring occasionally, until melted and combined. Remove the saucepan from the heat and leave to cool slightly. Sift the flour and ground ginger together into the butter mixture and beat until smooth. Spoon 2 teaspoons of the mixture onto the prepared baking sheet, spacing them well apart. Bake in the preheated oven for 8 minutes until pale golden brown. Keep the remaining mixture warm. Meanwhile, oil the handle of a wooden spoon.

2 Remove the baking sheet from the oven and leave to stand for 1 minute so that the brandy snaps firm up slightly. Remove one with a palette knife and immediately curl it around the handle of the wooden spoon. Once set, carefully slide it off the handle and transfer to a wire rack to cool completely. Repeat with the other brandy snap. Bake the remaining mixture and shape in the same way, using a cool baking sheet each time. Do not be tempted to cook more, or the rounds will set before you have time to shape them. When all the brandy snaps are cool, store in an airtight container.

3 To serve, spoon the whipped cream into a piping bag fitted with a star nozzle. Fill the brandy snaps with cream from both ends.

Cinnamon Poached
FRUIT

Serves 6

- 115 g/4 oz dried apricots
- 115 g/4 oz dried figs, halved
- 150 g/5½ oz Medjool dates, stoned and halved lengthways
- 115 g/4 oz sultanas
- 2 cinnamon sticks
- 2 star anise
- 5 cardamom pods, crushed
- 1 tbsp water

- 500 ml/18 fl oz Beaumes de Venise or other dessert wine
- seeds from 1 pomegranate, to garnish
- mascarpone cheese or crème fraîche, to serve

Almond thins
- 125 g/4½ oz ground almonds
- 175 g/6 oz unrefined caster sugar
- 3 tbsp finely grated orange rind
- 50 g/1¾ oz plain flour
- 3 large egg whites
- 50 g/1¾ oz flaked almonds, toasted
- 2 tbsp white icing sugar

1 The day before you want to serve, put all the fruit in a saucepan with the cinnamon sticks, star anise and cardamom pods. Add the water and wine, heat very gently to a simmer and poach for 5 minutes. Remove from the heat and remove the cardamom pods and star anise, but leave in the cinnamon sticks. Leave to cool completely, then cover and chill overnight in the refrigerator.

2 Preheat the oven to 180°C/350°F/Gas Mark 4. Line two baking sheets with baking paper. To make the biscuits, put the ground almonds in a bowl, add 100 g/3½ oz of the caster sugar, the orange rind and flour and stir well. In a separate bowl, whisk the egg whites until they form soft peaks, then whisk in the remaining caster sugar until the mixture is glossy and stiff. Fold the egg whites into the almond mixture.

3 Place teaspoonfuls of the mixture, spaced well apart, on the prepared baking sheets, then sprinkle over the almonds. Bake in the preheated oven for 12 minutes until puffed up and beginning to brown. Dust with the icing sugar and leave to cool for 10 minutes before transferring to a wire rack to cool completely.

4 To serve, remove the cinnamon sticks from the poached fruit and divide between six stemmed glasses. Spoon over a little mascarpone cheese and garnish with the pomegranate seeds. Serve with the almond thins.

PAVLOVA

Serves 4

- 6 egg whites
- pinch of cream of tartar
- pinch of salt
- 275 g/9¾ oz caster sugar
- 600 ml/1 pint double cream
- 1 tsp vanilla extract
- 2 kiwi fruits, peeled and sliced
- 250 g/9 oz strawberries, hulled and sliced
- 3 ripe peaches, sliced
- 1 ripe mango, peeled and sliced
- 2 tbsp orange liqueur, such as Cointreau
- fresh mint leaves, to garnish

1 Preheat the oven to 110°C/225°F/Gas Mark ¼ . Line three baking sheets with baking paper, then draw a 22-cm/8½-inch circle in the centre of each one. Beat the egg whites into stiff peaks. Mix in the cream of tartar and salt. Gradually add 200 g/7 oz of the sugar. Beat for 2 minutes until glossy.

2 Fill a piping bag with the meringue mixture and pipe enough to fill each circle, doming them slightly in the centre. Bake in the preheated oven for 1 hour. Remove from the oven and leave to cool.

3 Whip together the cream and vanilla extract with the remaining sugar. Put the fruit into a separate bowl and stir in the liqueur. Put one meringue circle onto a plate, then spread over a third of the sugared cream. Spread over a third of the fruit, then top with a meringue circle. Spread over another third of cream, then another third of fruit. Top with the last meringue circle. Spread over the remaining cream, followed by the rest of the fruit. Garnish with mint leaves and serve.

Chocolate Chestnut
ROULADE

Serves 6

- 6 large eggs, separated
- 150 g/5½ oz unrefined caster sugar
- ½ tsp vanilla or chocolate extract
- 50 g/1¾ oz cocoa powder
- icing sugar, for dusting
- 250 ml/9 fl oz double cream
- 250 g/9 oz sweetened chestnut purée
- 2 tbsp brandy
- 70 g/2½ oz cooked peeled chestnuts, chopped

1 Preheat the oven to 180°C/350°F/Gas Mark 4. Line a 23 x 45-cm (9 x 17¾-inch) Swiss roll tin with baking paper.

2 Using an electric whisk, beat the egg yolks, caster sugar and vanilla extract together in a bowl for 10 minutes, or until doubled in volume and pale and fluffy. In a separate bowl, whisk the egg whites until they form soft peaks. Fold a tablespoonful of egg whites into the egg yolk mixture, then gently fold in the remaining egg whites and the cocoa powder.

3 Spoon the cake mixture into the prepared tin and smooth the surface with a palette knife. Bake in the preheated oven for 20 minutes until risen. Leave to cool in the tin.

4 Put a large piece of baking paper over a clean tea towel and dust with icing sugar. Invert the sponge on to the baking paper and carefully peel away the lining paper. In a clean bowl, whisk the cream until stiff, then stir in the chestnut purée and the brandy. Spread over the sponge, leaving a 2.5-cm/1-inch margin around the edges, and scatter over the chestnuts. Using one end of the tea towel, carefully roll up the roulade. Dust with more icing sugar.

Frosted Christmas
BROWNIES

Makes 16

- 115 g/4 oz plain chocolate, broken into pieces
- 200 g/7 oz butter, plus extra for greasing
- 85 g/3 oz pecan nut halves
- 250 g/9 oz caster sugar
- 4 eggs, beaten
- 225 g/8 oz plain flour
- 2 tsp ground cinnamon
- 55 g/2 oz white chocolate, broken into pieces
- 2 tbsp milk
- 115 g/4 oz icing sugar

1 Preheat the oven to 180°C/350°F/Gas Mark 4. Grease a 23-cm/9-inch shallow square cake tin.

2 Melt the plain chocolate and 175 g/6 oz of the butter in a heatproof bowl, set over a pan of gently simmering water. Remove from the heat and allow to cool slightly.

3 Set 16 pecan halves to one side for decoration and chop the rest. Beat together the caster sugar and eggs with a whisk until thick and creamy. Then fold in the chocolate mixture, flour, cinnamon and chopped pecans.

4 Transfer the mixture to the prepared tin and bake in the preheated oven for 35–40 minutes until just firm to the touch. Allow to cool in the tin.

5 Melt the remaining butter and white chocolate in a heatproof bowl, set over a pan of gently simmering water. Remove from the heat and beat in the milk and icing sugar. Spread this mixture over the cooled brownies. Allow to set for 30 minutes then cut into 16 squares and top each square with a pecan half.

Gingerbread
HOUSE

Makes 1 house
- 400 g/14 oz self-raising flour
- 125 g/4½ oz unsalted butter, chilled and diced, plus extra for greasing
- 125 g/4½ oz light muscovado sugar
- 1½ tsp ground ginger
- ½ tsp ground cloves
- 1 tsp ground cinnamon
- 125 g/4½ oz black treacle
- 1 large egg, beaten
- 500 g/1 lb 2 oz easy-spread white royal icing
- soft icing, for piping
- sweets, biscuits and edible silver balls, to decorate

1 Grease two baking sheets and line with baking paper. Sift the flour into a large bowl and rub in the remaining butter until the mixture resembles breadcrumbs. Stir in the sugar and spices. In a separate bowl, whisk the treacle with the egg and pour on to the dry ingredients. Stir well to combine and mix to a smooth dough. Wrap in clingfilm and chill in the refrigerator for 30 minutes.

2 Preheat the oven to 200°C/400°F/Gas Mark 6. Divide the dough into six pieces. You will need to roll each dough out to 5 mm/¼ inch thick and cut six pieces for the house – the easiest method is to use cardboard or paper templates. Cut two pieces for the side walls (16 x 10 cm/6¼ x 4 inches), two for the end walls (12 cm/4½ inches wide and 17 cm/6½ inches at the tip of the 'gable') and two for the roof (18 x 12 cm/7 x 4½ inches). Cut out a window in one of the side walls and a door in the front.

3 Lay the pieces of dough on the prepared baking sheets and bake in the preheated oven for 10–12 minutes until slightly risen and evenly cooked. Leave to cool on the baking sheets, then transfer to a wire rack to cool completely.

4 To assemble the house, spread a line of royal icing on a cake board and position a 'wall' on it. Using small glasses to support it, spread a little more icing on the ends and board and attach the other 'walls'. Leave the house to set for 30 minutes and make sure that it is standing securely before adding more icing to attach the roof pieces. Again, leave to set before spreading on more icing over the roof, pulling the icing over the edge to create 'icicles'. Use soft icing to pipe along the joins. Decorate the house with sweets, biscuits and silver balls.

122

Christmas Frosted
GINGER CAKE

Serves 6–8

- 175 g/6 oz unsalted butter, softened, plus extra for greasing
- 175 g/6 oz unrefined caster sugar
- 3 large eggs, beaten
- 1 tbsp black treacle
- 2 tbsp ginger syrup

- 225 g/8 oz self-raising flour
- 1 tsp ground ginger
- 1 tsp ground mixed spice
- 1 tbsp ground almonds
- 2 tbsp full-fat milk
- 70 g/2½ oz stem ginger, chopped

- edible gold or silver balls, to decorate

Icing
- 225 g/8 oz icing sugar
- 1 tsp ginger syrup

1 Preheat the oven to 160°C/325°F/Gas Mark 3. Grease a 15 x 25-cm/6 x 10-inch cake tin and line with baking paper.

2 Cream the butter and caster sugar in a large bowl until pale and fluffy. Put the eggs and treacle into a jug with the ginger syrup and whisk together. Sift the flour and spices on to a plate. Alternately, add a little of the egg mixture and then a spoonful of the flour mixture to the butter and sugar mixture until you have used up both. Add the almonds and milk and stir together until you have a smooth mixture. Fold in the stem ginger pieces.

3 Spoon the cake mixture into the prepared tin, smooth the surface with a palette knife and bake in the preheated oven for 45–50 minutes until well risen and firm to the touch. Leave to cool in the tin for 10 minutes, then turn out on to a wire rack to cool completely.

4 To make the icing, put the icing sugar in a large bowl. Beat in the ginger syrup and just enough cold water to make a thick icing – be careful not to add too much water, too quickly. Remove the cake from the tin and spread the icing over the top, letting it run down the sides. Decorate with edible gold or silver balls.

Brown Sugar & Cinnamon
ROLLS

Makes 12

- 450 g/1 lb plain flour, plus extra for dusting
- 1½ tsp salt
- 30 g/1 oz unrefined caster sugar
- 2 tsp easy-blend dried yeast
- 250 ml/9 fl oz tepid full-fat milk
- vegetable oil, for oiling
- 85 g/3 oz muscovado sugar
- 1½ tsp ground cinnamon
- 1 egg, beaten

Cook's note...

For an easy festive breakfast, you can make this dough ahead of time and freeze it – simply thaw and brush with the egg and sugar before baking and serving.

1 Mix the flour, salt, caster sugar and yeast together in a large bowl. Stir in the milk to form a dough. Knead the dough on a floured work surface until smooth and pliable. Put in a clean bowl, cover the bowl and leave to prove in a warm place for 2 hours.

2 Meanwhile, oil two baking sheets. Knock back the dough and knead briefly again on a floured surface, then roll out to a rectangle measuring 30 x 24 cm/ 12 x 9½ inches. Mix 55 g/2 oz of the muscovado sugar with the cinnamon and sprinkle over the surface. Press into the dough, then roll up the dough tightly like a Swiss roll and cut into 12 evenly sized pieces. Lay each piece on its side on the prepared baking sheets, cover with a clean tea towel and leave to prove in a warm place for 30 minutes. Preheat the oven to 200°C/400°F/Gas Mark 6.

3 Brush the rolls with the egg and sprinkle over the remaining muscovado sugar. Bake in the preheated oven for 12–15 minutes until golden – be careful not to overcook and burn them. Transfer to a wire rack to cool.

PANETTONE

Serves 8

- 10 cardamom pods
- 15 g/½ oz butter, plus extra for greasing
- 300 g/10½ oz strong plain flour, plus extra for dusting
- 2 tbsp caster sugar
- ½ tsp easy-blend dried yeast
- 1 tsp salt
- grated rind of 1 lemon
- 1 tsp vanilla extract
- 150 ml/5 fl oz milk
- 2 egg yolks
- 55 g/2 oz mixed peel, chopped
- 115 g/4 oz sultanas

1 Grease a 17.5-cm/7-inch cake tin. Crush the cardamom pods lightly in a pestle and mortar and discard the shells. Grind the cardamom seeds to a powder.

2 Rub the butter into the flour and add the sugar, yeast, salt and cardamom powder. Stir to mix evenly. Add the lemon rind, vanilla extract, milk, egg yolks and mix together with a wooden spoon to make a soft dough.

3 Turn the dough out onto a floured work surface and knead for 10 minutes. Return the dough to the bowl, cover with clingfilm and leave to prove in a warm place for 2 hours or until doubled in size.

4 Return the dough to the lightly floured work surface and knock back the dough. Knead in the mixed peel and sultanas until evenly distributed. Transfer to the prepared tin and cover with clingfilm. Leave to prove again for a further 2 hours or until doubled in size.

5 Preheat the oven to 150°C/300°F/Gas Mark 2. Remove the clingfilm from the prepared tin and bake in the preheated oven for 1 hour until dark golden brown. Allow to cool in the tin for 20 minutes before running a palette knife around the tin to loosen. Transfer the cake to a wire rack to cool completely.

Cranberry
MUFFINS

Makes 18

- butter, for greasing
- 225 g/8 oz plain flour
- 2 tsp baking powder
- ½ tsp salt
- 50 g/1¾ oz caster sugar
- 55 g/2 oz unsalted butter, melted
- 2 eggs, lightly beaten
- 175 ml/6 fl oz milk
- 115 g/4 oz fresh cranberries
- 50 g/1¾ oz Parmesan cheese, freshly grated

1 Preheat the oven to 200°C/400°F/Gas Mark 6. Grease two 9-cup muffin tins.

2 Sift the flour, baking powder and salt into a bowl. Stir in the sugar. Combine the butter, eggs and milk in a separate bowl, then pour into the bowl of dry ingredients. Stir until all of the ingredients are evenly combined, then stir in the fresh cranberries.

3 Divide the mixture evenly between the prepared 18 cups in the muffin tins. Sprinkle the grated Parmesan cheese over the top. Bake in the preheated oven for 20 minutes until risen and golden.

4 Remove the muffins from the oven and leave to cool slightly in the tins. Put the muffins on a wire rack and leave to cool completely.

Chocolate
FLORENTINES

Makes 20

- 25 g/1 oz unsalted butter, plus extra for greasing
- 70 g/2½ oz unrefined caster sugar
- 15 g/½ oz plain flour, plus extra for dusting
- 4 tbsp double cream
- 50 g/1¾ oz whole blanched almonds, roughly chopped
- 50 g/1¾ oz flaked almonds, toasted
- 50 g/1¾ oz mixed peel, chopped
- 50 g/1¾ oz undyed glacé cherries, chopped

Cook's note...
Use whole candied peel if you can find it and chop it yourself. If you don't like ginger, replace it with angelica or dyed green cherries.

- 50 g/1¾ oz preserved stem ginger, drained and chopped
- 70 g/2½ oz plain chocolate, broken into pieces
- 70 g/2½ oz white chocolate, broken into pieces

1 Preheat the oven to 190°C/375°F/Gas Mark 5. Grease two baking sheets and dust with flour, shaking to remove any excess.

2 Put the remaining butter, sugar and flour in a small saucepan and heat gently, stirring well, until the mixture has melted. Gradually add the cream, stirring constantly, then add all the remaining ingredients, except the chocolate, and stir thoroughly. Remove from the heat and leave to cool.

3 Drop 5 teaspoons of the mixture onto each of the prepared baking sheets, spaced well apart, then flatten with the back of a spoon. Bake in the preheated oven for 12–15 minutes. Leave the biscuits to harden on the sheets for 2–3 minutes before transferring to a wire rack. Repeat with the remaining mixture, again using the two baking sheets.

4 When the biscuits are completely cool, put the plain chocolate in a heatproof bowl, set the bowl over a saucepan of gently simmering water and heat until melted. Using a teaspoon, spread the base of 10 of the biscuits with the melted chocolate and place chocolate-side up on a wire rack to set. Repeat with the white chocolate and the remaining 10 biscuits.

Chocolate
TRUFFLES

Makes 40–50
- 225 g/8 oz plain chocolate, minimum 70% cocoa solids
- 175 ml/6 fl oz whipping cream
- cocoa powder, icing sugar or chopped toasted almonds, for coating

Cook's note...
You can also add other flavours to the truffles – add a little brandy, Calvados or dark rum to the mixture before you leave it to set. The truffles could also be covered in milk chocolate or white chocolate – a mixture looks inviting when boxed as a gift.

1 Roughly chop the chocolate and put in a large heatproof bowl. Put the cream in a saucepan and bring up to boiling point. Pour over the chocolate and whisk until smooth. Leave to cool at room temperature for 1½–2 hours.

2 Cover two baking sheets with clingfilm or baking paper. Using a teaspoon, take bite-sized scoops of the chocolate mixture and roll in cocoa powder, icing sugar or chopped almonds to form balls, then place on the prepared baking sheets and chill in the refrigerator until set.

Christmas Spiced
PANCAKES

Serves 4

- 150 g/5½ oz plain white flour
- 1½ tsp baking powder
- pinch of salt
- 1 tsp mixed spice
- 250 ml/9 fl oz milk
- 1 large egg
- 2 tbsp melted butter
- 100 g/3½ oz cranberries, chopped
- 40 g/1½ oz mixed peel, chopped
- 25 g/1 oz mixed nuts, chopped
- sunflower oil, for greasing

Syrup

- 2 tbsp soft dark brown sugar
- 50 ml/2 fl oz water
- 3 tbsp dark rum
- 1 tsp vanilla extract

1 Sift the flour, baking powder, salt and mixed spice into a bowl. Add the milk, egg and butter and whisk to a smooth batter. Stir in the cranberries, mixed peel and nuts and leave to stand for 5 minutes.

2 Lightly grease a griddle pan or frying pan and heat over a medium heat. Spoon tablespoons of batter onto the pan to make oval shapes, and cook until bubbles appear on the surface.

3 Turn over with a palette knife and cook the other side until golden brown. Repeat this process using the remaining batter, while keeping the cooked pancakes warm.

4 For the syrup, place the sugar and water in a small saucepan and heat over a low heat, stirring, until the sugar dissolves. Bring to the boil and boil for 1 minute, then add the rum and vanilla extract and return to the boil. Remove from the heat.

5 Spoon the syrup over the pancakes and serve immediately.

Orange Ice Cream with Almond
PRALINE

Serves 6

- 1 large orange
- 100 g/3½ oz granulated sugar
- 175 ml/6 fl oz water
- ½ tsp orange flower water
- butter, for greasing
- 225 g/8 oz caster sugar
- 125 g/4½ oz flaked almonds, toasted

Ice cream
- 1 vanilla pod
- 300 ml/10 fl oz single cream
- 4 large egg yolks
- 2 tsp custard powder
- 50 g/1¾ oz caster sugar
- 300 ml/10 fl oz crème fraîche

1 Cut away the flesh of the orange, leaving the rind and a little pith. Cut the rind into 5-cm/2-inch pieces. Put the granulated sugar and 100 ml/3½ fl oz of the water in a saucepan and heat gently, stirring, until the sugar has dissolved. Bring to the boil and add the orange flower water and orange rind. Reduce the heat and simmer gently for 15–20 minutes. Leave the rind to cool in the syrup, then lift out onto greaseproof paper to cool completely and roughly chop.

2 Grease a piece of foil with butter. Put the caster sugar in a pan with the remaining water and heat gently, stirring, until the sugar has dissolved. Bring to a simmer, swirling the saucepan, and cook until the syrup reaches a caramel-orange colour. Remove from the heat and tip in the almonds. Stir, pour onto the greased foil and spread out. Leave to cool and harden, then break into shards.

3 To make the ice cream, slit the vanilla pod open and scrape out the seeds. Put the pod and cream in a saucepan and heat gently. Put the vanilla seeds, egg yolks, custard powder and sugar in a heatproof bowl and whisk until smooth. When the cream is about to boil, remove the vanilla pod and, whisking constantly, pour the cream over the egg yolk mixture. Continuing to stir, pour the mixture into the saucepan and bring to the boil. Reduce the heat and simmer until thickened. Plunge the saucepan's base into a bowl of iced water, then stir until cool. Fold in the crème fraîche and chopped orange peel. When cold, pour into an ice-cream machine and churn according to the manufacturer's instructions. Alternatively, pour into a freezerproof container, cover and freeze for 12 hours. Remove from the freezer and beat to break down any ice crystals. Re-freeze and beat as before, then re-freeze until solid. Serve with the praline.

Snowflake Christmas
WHOOPIE PIES

Makes 14
- 200 g/7 oz plain flour
- 2 tsp baking powder
- large pinch of salt
- 55 g/2 oz ground almonds
- 115 g/4 oz butter, softened
- 150 g/5½ oz caster sugar, plus extra for sprinkling
- 1 large egg, beaten
- 1 tsp almond extract
- 100 ml/4 fl oz milk
- 1 tbsp edible silver balls, to decorate

Buttercream filling
- 150 g/5½ oz unsalted butter, softened
- 8 tbsp double cream
- 280 g/10 oz icing sugar, sifted

Icing
- 115 g/4 oz icing sugar
- 1–2 tbsp warm water

1 Preheat the oven to 180°C/350°F/Gas Mark 4. Line two or three large baking sheets with baking paper. Sift together the plain flour, baking powder and salt. Stir in the ground almonds.

2 Place the butter and caster sugar in a large bowl and beat until pale and fluffy. Beat in the egg and almond extract, followed by half the flour mixture then the milk. Stir in the rest of the flour mixture and beat until well mixed.

3 Pipe or spoon 28 mounds of the mixture onto the prepared baking sheets, spaced well apart. Bake in the preheated oven, one sheet at a time, for 10–12 minutes until risen and just firm to the touch. Cool for 5 minutes then, using a palette knife, transfer to a wire rack and leave to cool completely.

4 For the filling, place the butter in a bowl and beat with an electric whisk for 2–3 minutes until pale and creamy. Beat in the cream then gradually beat in the icing sugar and continue beating for 2–3 minutes until the buttercream is very light and fluffy. For the icing, sift the icing sugar into a bowl and gradually stir in enough water to make a smooth, thick icing.

5 To assemble, spread the buttercream on the flat side of half of the cakes. Top with the rest of the cakes. Spoon the icing into a small paper piping bag, snip the end and pipe snowflake patterns on the top of the whoopie pies. Decorate with silver balls and sprinkle with caster sugar. Leave to set.

Traditional
BRANDY BUTTER

....

Serves 6–8

- 115 g/4 oz unsalted butter,
  at room temperature
- 55 g/2 oz caster sugar
- 55 g/2 oz icing sugar, sifted
- 3 tbsp brandy

1 Cream the butter in a bowl until it is very smooth and soft. Gradually beat in both types of sugar. Add the brandy, a little at a time, beating well after each addition and taking care not to let the mixture curdle.

2 Spread out the butter on a sheet of foil, cover and chill in the refrigerator until firm. Keep chilled until ready to serve.

5

Christmas

COOKIES

Fun and Festive
BAKING

Christmas cookie baking is easy, fun and something you can do with children… and results in a lot of scrumptious treats! The joy of making cookies with the children comes from the fact that they can get involved in every stage of the process – meaning the finished result will truly seem to be theirs.

First, clear an afternoon and set out all the ingredients on a table. Take turns to mix up the dough and involve the children in deciding which cookies you're going to make. As the basic recipes are all similar, baking several batches in one go isn't too hard.

Build up a collection of Christmas and normal cookie cutters – charity shops and car-boot sales can be particularly rich sources. Snapping them up as and when you see them through the year means that, come December, you should be in possession of a wide range. Failing that, a little imagination with the decorating can see even the most basic gingerbread man transformed into a snowman or Santa.

The best part of making cookies is definitely the decorating (apart from the eating, obviously!). Putting your own – and more importantly, letting your children put their own – personal stamp on your creations is what makes them so much better than anything bought off the shelves. Mix up as many different colours of icing sugar as you can, set out bowls of hundreds-and-thousands, chocolate drops, milk buttons, jelly babies… and whatever else takes your fancy. Let your imagination run away with you.

Baking cookies is all about sharing – sharing the fun of making them, sharing the treat of eating them, and sharing the joy of giving them. They're like Christmas itself – with chocolate buttons and icing sugar on top! Why not make these gift tags to attach to your cookies gifts? For this project, you will need a craft knife, steel-edged ruler, cutting mat, hole punch and double-sided tape.

Gift Tags

Materials

- 300 gsm white, green or red card
- red and sage-green felt
- sewing needle and deep-red embroidery thread
- holly leaves
- deep-red raw-silk fabric scraps
- red ribbon
- craft equipment (see bottom of page 146)

1 Choose any colour card to make your gift tags to the size you require. Cut out a rectangular shape with a craft knife and steel-edged ruler on a cutting mat. Punch a hole in the corner. Repeat this procedure until you have as many rectangular cards as you need (one card is needed per tag).

2 Attach the red felt to half of the cards and the green felt to the other half of the cards with double-sided tape. Trim with the craft knife.

3 Using the sewing needle and embroidery thread, sew holly leaves to the felt side of the red felt cards with one cross-stitch, tying the thread at the back and trimming the excess.

4 Cut three small squares of the silk and, using double-sided tape, adhere to the felt side of the green felt cards, overlapping them at jaunty angles. Add a small sage-green felt heart to one of the silk squares with double-sided tape.

5 Carefully cut the punched holes in the tags with the craft knife, thread a length of red ribbon through each hole and make a knot in the ribbon.

Snowflake
GINGERBREAD

Makes 30

- 350 g/12 oz plain flour, plus extra for dusting
- 1 tbsp ground ginger
- 1 tsp bicarbonate of soda
- 100 g/3½ oz butter, softened, plus extra for greasing
- 175 g/6 oz soft brown sugar
- 1 egg, beaten
- 4 tbsp golden syrup

To decorate
- 115 g/4 oz icing sugar
- 2 tbsp lemon juice

1 Preheat the oven to 180°C/350°F/Gas Mark 4. Grease three baking sheets.

2 Sift the flour, ginger and bicarbonate of soda together in a bowl. Add the butter and rub into the flour until the mixture resembles fine breadcrumbs, then stir in the brown sugar.

3 In another bowl, beat together the egg and golden syrup with a fork. Pour this mixture into the flour mixture and mix to make a smooth dough, kneading lightly with your hands.

4 Roll the dough out on a lightly floured work surface to about 5 mm/¼ inch thick and cut into shapes using a snowflake-shaped cutter. Transfer the cookies to the prepared baking sheets.

5 Bake in the preheated oven for 10 minutes until golden brown. Remove the cookies from the oven and allow to cool for 5 minutes before transferring, using a palette knife, to a wire rack to cool completely.

6 Once the cookies are cool, mix together the icing sugar and lemon juice until smooth and place into a piping bag fitted with a very small nozzle. Pipe snowflake shapes onto each biscuit, using the icing. Leave to set for a few hours.

Eggnog
COOKIES

Makes 35

- 1 egg
- 175 g/6 oz caster sugar
- 6 tbsp rum
- 3 tbsp milk
- 150 g/5½ oz butter, softened, plus extra for greasing
- 1 tsp vanilla extract
- 2 egg yolks
- 280 g/10 oz plain flour
- 1 tsp baking powder
- ¾ tsp ground nutmeg
- 175 g/6 oz icing sugar

1 Preheat the oven to 160°C/325°F/Gas Mark 3. Grease two baking sheets. To make the eggnog mixture, beat together the egg, 25 g/1 oz of the caster sugar, rum and milk until frothy. Set aside.

2 In a large bowl, cream the rest of the caster sugar and 140 g/5 oz of the butter until light and fluffy. Beat in the vanilla extract and egg yolks until smooth.

3 Sift together the flour, baking powder and ½ teaspoon of nutmeg into the mixture and beat in 100 ml/4 fl oz of the eggnog mixture until just combined.

4 Place heaped teaspoonfuls of the mixture on the prepared baking sheets, spaced well apart. Flatten slightly with damp fingers and bake in the preheated oven for 20–25 minutes, or until the bottom of the cookies turn golden.

5 Leave to cool for 5 minutes on the baking sheets and then transfer to wire racks to cool completely.

6 Once the cookies are cool, beat together the icing sugar, remaining butter and the remaining eggnog mixture to make a soft, spreadable icing. Ice the cookies and sprinkle with a little nutmeg on top. Leave to set for a few hours.

Spiced
RUM COOKIES

Makes 18

- 175 g/6 oz unsalted butter, softened, plus extra for greasing
- 175 g/6 oz dark muscovado sugar
- 225 g/8 oz plain flour
- pinch of salt
- ½ tsp bicarbonate of soda
- 1 tsp ground cinnamon
- ¼ tsp ground coriander
- ½ tsp ground nutmeg
- ¼ tsp ground cloves
- 2 tbsp dark rum

1 Preheat the oven to 180°C/350°F/Gas Mark 4. Grease two baking sheets.

2 Cream together the butter and sugar and whisk until light and fluffy. Sift together the flour, salt, bicarbonate of soda, cinnamon, coriander, nutmeg and cloves into the creamed mixture.

3 Stir the dark rum into the creamed mixture. Place 18 spoonfuls of the dough onto the prepared baking sheets, spaced well apart. Flatten each one slightly with the back of a spoon.

4 Bake in a preheated oven for 10–12 minutes until golden. Leave the biscuits to cool and crisp on wire racks before serving.

CHEQUERBOARDS

Makes about 20

- 225 g/8 oz butter, softened
- 140 g/5 oz caster sugar
- 1 egg yolk, lightly beaten
- 2 tsp vanilla extract
- 280 g/10 oz plain flour
- pinch of salt
- 1 tsp ground ginger
- 1 tbsp finely grated orange rind
- 1 tbsp cocoa powder
- 1 egg white, lightly beaten

1 Place the butter and sugar in a large bowl and beat together until light and fluffy, then beat in the egg yolk and vanilla extract. Sift together the flour and salt into the mixture and stir until combined.

2 Divide the dough in half. Add the ginger and orange rind to one half and mix well. Shape the dough into a log 15 cm/6 inches long. Flatten the sides and top to square off the log to 5 cm/2 inches high. Wrap in clingfilm and chill in the refrigerator for 30–60 minutes.

3 Sift the cocoa into the other half of the dough and mix well. Shape into a flattened log exactly the same size as the first one, wrap in clingfilm and chill in the refrigerator for 30–60 minutes.

4 Unwrap the two doughs and cut each log lengthways into three slices. Cut each slice lengthways into three strips. Brush the strips with egg white and stack them in threes, alternating the colours, so they are the same shape as the original logs. Wrap in clingfilm and chill for 30–60 minutes.

5 Preheat the oven to 190°C/375°F/Gas Mark 5. Line two large baking sheets with baking paper.

6 Unwrap the logs and cut into slices with a sharp serrated knife, then place the cookies on the prepared baking sheets, spaced well apart. Bake in the preheated oven for 12–15 minutes, or until firm. Leave to cool for 5–10 minutes, then transfer the cookies to wire racks to cool completely.

Santa
SUGAR COOKIES

Makes 40

- 350 g/12 oz plain flour, plus extra for dusting
- 1 tsp baking powder
- ¼ tsp salt
- 115 g/4 oz butter, softened, plus extra for greasing
- 175 g/6 oz caster sugar
- 1 egg, beaten
- 2½ tsp vanilla extract
- 1 tbsp milk

To decorate
- 225 g/8 oz icing sugar
- 1 egg white
- ½ tsp glycerine
- glycerine-based red and black food colouring

1 Grease four baking sheets. Sift together the flour, baking powder and salt together in a bowl. In a separate bowl, cream the butter and the caster sugar together until light and fluffy. Beat in the egg, 2 teaspoons of the vanilla extract and milk until smooth and then mix in the flour mixture to form a soft dough. Cover the dough with clingfilm and chill in the refrigerator for 30 minutes.

2 Preheat the oven to 180°C/350°F/Gas Mark 4. Roll out the chilled dough on a lightly floured work surface to 5 mm/¼ inch thick. Use a Santa-shaped cutter to cut out shapes from the dough. Transfer the cookies to the prepared baking sheets. Bake the cookies in the preheated oven for 10 minutes until golden brown. Remove from the oven and allow to cool for 5 minutes before transferring, using a palette knife, to a wire rack to cool completely.

3 Once the cookies are cool, whisk together the icing sugar, egg white, remaining vanilla extract and glycerine with an electric whisk for 5 minutes until stiff and glossy. Colour one third of the icing sugar mixture red and colour 2 tablespoons of the mixture black. Leave the rest of the mixture as white icing. Apply the red icing evenly with a small palette knife to create Santa's hat and pipe eyes in black icing using a fine nozzle.

4 Place the white icing in a piping bag fitted with a small star-shaped nozzle to create the fur cuff, eyebrows, moustache and bobble on Santa's hat. Apply the remainder of the icing using a swirling action with a small palette knife to create his beard. Leave to set for a few hours.

Reindeer
COOKIES

Makes 25

- 10 cardamom pods
- 100 g/3½ oz butter, softened, plus extra for greasing
- 55 g/2 oz caster sugar
- 1 egg, beaten
- finely grated rind of ½ orange
- 225 g/8 oz plain flour, plus extra for dusting
- 25 g/1 oz cornflour
- ½ tsp baking powder

To decorate

- 90 g/3¼ oz icing sugar
- 4 tsp lemon juice
- glycerine-based red food colouring
- 25 edible silver balls

1 Crush the cardamom pods lightly in a pestle and mortar and discard the shells. Grind the cardamom seeds to a powder. Beat together the butter and caster sugar in a bowl with a whisk until creamy, then gradually beat in the egg, orange rind and cardamom powder.

2 Sift together the flour, cornflour and baking powder into the mixture and stir with a wooden spoon to form a soft dough. Wrap the dough in clingfilm and chill in the refrigerator for 30 minutes.

3 Preheat the oven to 180°C/350°F/Gas Mark 4. Grease three baking sheets. Roll out the chilled dough on a lightly floured work surface to 3 mm/⅛ inch thick. Cut out shapes using a reindeer-shaped cutter, and place on the prepared baking sheets. Re-knead and re-roll trimmings and cut out more shapes until all the dough is used up.

4 Bake in the preheated oven for 15 minutes, until just golden. Allow to cool for 5 minutes before transferring to a wire rack to cool completely.

5 Mix together the icing sugar and lemon juice until smooth. Spoon 2 tablespoons of the mixture into a separate mixing bowl and colour it with the red food colouring. Spoon the rest of the icing into a piping bag fitted with a fine nozzle and pipe antlers, hooves, tail, collar and a saddle in white icing on the cookies. Pipe a nose using the red icing. For the eye, fix a silver ball using a blob of icing.

Sugar
COOKIE HEARTS

Makes about 30
- 225 g/8 oz butter, softened
- 280 g/10 oz caster sugar
- 1 egg yolk, lightly beaten
- 2 tsp vanilla extract
- 250 g/9 oz plain flour
- 25 g/1 oz cocoa powder
- pinch of salt
- 3–4 food colouring pastes
- 100 g/3½ oz plain chocolate,
  broken into pieces

1 Place the butter and half the sugar in a large bowl and beat together until light and fluffy, then beat in the egg yolk and vanilla extract. Sift together the flour, cocoa and salt into the mixture and stir until combined. Halve the dough, shape into balls, wrap in clingfilm and chill for 30–60 minutes.

2 Preheat the oven to 190°C/375°F/Gas Mark 5. Line two large baking sheets with baking paper. Unwrap the dough and roll out between two sheets of baking paper. Cut out cookies with a heart-shaped cutter and place them on the prepared baking sheets, spaced well apart. Bake in the preheated oven for 10–15 minutes, or until firm. Leave to cool on the baking sheets for 5–10 minutes, then transfer to wire racks to cool completely.

3 Meanwhile, divide the remaining sugar among four small plastic bags or bowls. Add a little food colouring paste to each and rub in until well mixed. Wear a plastic glove if mixing in bowls to prevent your hands from getting stained. Place the chocolate in a heatproof bowl, set the bowl over a saucepan of gently simmering water and heat until melted. Leave to cool slightly.

4 Leave the cookies on the racks. Spread the melted chocolate over them and sprinkle with the coloured sugar. Leave to set.

Cinnamon & Chocolate
CHIP COOKIES

Makes about 30

- 225 g/8 oz butter, softened
- 140 g/5 oz caster sugar
- 1 egg yolk, lightly beaten
- 2 tsp orange extract
- 280 g/10 oz plain flour
- pinch of salt
- 100 g/3½ oz plain chocolate chips

Cinnamon coating

- 1½ tbsp caster sugar
- 1½ tbsp ground cinnamon

1 Preheat the oven to 190°C/375°F/Gas Mark 5. Line two baking sheets with baking paper.

2 Put the butter and sugar into a bowl and mix well with a wooden spoon, then beat in the egg yolk and orange extract. Sift together the flour and salt into the mixture, add the chocolate chips and stir until thoroughly combined.

3 For the cinnamon coating, mix together the sugar and cinnamon in a shallow dish. Scoop out tablespoons of the cookie dough, roll them into balls, then roll them in the cinnamon mixture to coat. Flatten the cookies slightly with your fingers and put them on the prepared baking sheets, spaced well apart.

4 Bake in the preheated oven for 12–15 minutes. Leave to cool on the baking sheets for 5–10 minutes, then, using a palette knife, carefully transfer to wire racks to cool completely.

Cranberry & Coconut
COOKIES

Makes about 30

- 225 g/8 oz butter, softened
- 140 g/5 oz caster sugar
- 1 egg yolk, lightly beaten
- 2 tsp vanilla extract
- 280 g/10 oz plain flour
- pinch of salt
- 40 g/1½ oz desiccated coconut
- 60 g/2¼ oz dried cranberries

1 Preheat the oven to 190°C/375°F/Gas Mark 5. Line two baking sheets with baking paper.

2 Put the butter and sugar into a bowl and mix well with a wooden spoon, then beat in the egg yolk and vanilla extract. Sift together the flour and salt into the mixture, add the coconut and cranberries and stir until thoroughly combined. Scoop up tablespoons of the dough and place in mounds on the prepared baking sheets, spaced well apart.

3 Bake in the preheated oven for 12–15 minutes, until golden brown. Leave to cool on the baking sheets for 5–10 minutes, then, using a palette knife, carefully transfer to wire racks to cool completely.

Cookie
CANDY CANES

Makes 40

- 350 g/12 oz plain flour, plus extra for dusting
- 1 tsp bicarbonate of soda
- 100 g/3½ oz butter, softened, plus extra for greasing
- 175 g/6 oz soft brown sugar
- 1 egg, beaten
- 1 tsp vanilla extract
- 4 tbsp golden syrup

To decorate
- 450 g/1 lb icing sugar
- 135 ml/4½ fl oz lemon juice
- glycerine-based red food colouring

1 Preheat the oven to 180°C/350°F/Gas Mark 4. Grease three baking sheets.

2 Sift the flour and bicarbonate of soda together in a bowl. Add the butter and rub into the flour until the mixture resembles fine breadcrumbs, then stir in the brown sugar. In another bowl, beat together the egg, vanilla extract and golden syrup with a fork. Pour this mixture into the flour blend and stir to make a smooth dough, kneading lightly with your hands.

3 Roll the dough out on a lightly floured work surface to about 5 mm/¼ inch thick and cut into shapes using a candy cane-shaped cutter. Transfer the cookies to the prepared baking sheets. Bake in the preheated oven for 10 minutes, until golden brown. Remove the cookies from the oven and allow to cool for 5 minutes, before transferring, using a palette knife, to a wire rack to cool completely.

4 Once the cookies are cool, mix together 280 g/10 oz of the icing sugar and 75 ml/2½ fl oz of the lemon juice until smooth. Spoon the mixture into a piping bag fitted with a very fine nozzle and pipe the icing around the edge of the cookies. Empty any remaining icing into a small bowl, colour it with the red food colouring and cover with clingfilm. Mix the remaining icing sugar with the remaining lemon juice until smooth and runny. Spoon this into the centre of each cookie and encourage it to the piped edge to flood each biscuit. Allow to set overnight. Spoon the red icing into a piping bag fitted with a very fine nozzle and pipe stripes, dots and swirls over the dry iced cookies.

Cinnamon & Caramel
COOKIES

Makes about 25

- 225 g/8 oz butter, softened
- 140 g/5 oz caster sugar
- 1 egg yolk, lightly beaten
- 1 tsp vanilla extract
- 280 g/10 oz plain flour
- 1 tsp ground cinnamon
- ½ tsp mixed spice
- pinch of salt
- 25–30 caramel sweets

1 Preheat the oven to 190°C/375°F/Gas Mark 5. Line two baking sheets with baking paper.

2 Put the butter and sugar into a bowl and mix well with a wooden spoon, then beat in the egg yolk and vanilla extract. Sift together the flour, cinnamon, mixed spice and salt into the mixture and stir until thoroughly combined.

3 Scoop up tablespoons of the mixture, shape into balls and place on the prepared baking sheets, spaced well apart. Bake in the preheated oven for 8 minutes. Place a caramel sweet on top of each cookie, return to the oven and bake for a further 6–7 minutes.

4 Remove from the oven and leave to cool on the baking sheets for 5–10 minutes. Using a palette knife, carefully transfer the cookies to wire racks to cool completely.

Apple &
SPICE COOKIES

Makes about 30

- 225 g/8 oz butter, softened
- 140 g/5 oz caster sugar
- 1 egg yolk, lightly beaten
- 2 tsp apple juice
- 280 g/10 oz plain flour
- ½ tsp ground cinnamon
- ½ tsp mixed spice
- pinch of salt
- 100 g/3½ oz dried apple, finely chopped

Apple filling
- 1 tbsp caster sugar
- 1 tbsp custard powder
- 125 ml/4 fl oz milk
- 5 tbsp apple sauce

1 Put the butter and sugar into a bowl and mix well with a wooden spoon, then beat in the egg yolk and apple juice. Sift together the flour, cinnamon, mixed spice and salt into the mixture, add the dried apple and stir until thoroughly combined. Halve the dough, shape into balls, wrap in clingfilm and chill in the refrigerator for 30–60 minutes.

2 Preheat the oven to 190°C/375°F/Gas Mark 5. Line two baking sheets with baking paper.

3 Unwrap the dough and roll out between two sheets of baking paper. Stamp out cookies with a 5-cm/2-inch square cutter and put them on the prepared baking sheets, spaced well apart. Bake in the preheated oven for 10–15 minutes, until light golden brown. Leave to cool on the baking sheets for 5–10 minutes, then, using a palette knife, carefully transfer to wire racks to cool completely.

4 To make the apple filling, mix together the sugar, custard powder and milk in a saucepan and bring to the boil, stirring constantly. Cook, stirring constantly, until thickened, then remove the pan from the heat and stir in the apple sauce. Cover the surface with clingfilm and leave to cool.

5 Spread the filling over half the cookies and top with the remainder.

Christmas
BELLS

Makes about 30

- 225 g/8 oz butter, softened
- 140 g/5 oz caster sugar
- finely grated rind of 1 lemon
- 1 egg yolk, lightly beaten
- 280 g/10 oz plain flour
- ½ tsp ground cinnamon
- pinch of salt
- 100 g/3½ oz plain chocolate chips

To decorate
- 2 tbsp lightly beaten egg white
- 2 tbsp lemon juice
- 225 g/8 oz icing sugar
- 30 edible silver balls
- food colouring pens

1 Put the butter, caster sugar and lemon rind into a bowl and mix well with a wooden spoon, then beat in the egg yolk. Sift together the flour, cinnamon and salt into the mixture, add the chocolate chips and stir until thoroughly combined. Halve the dough, shape into balls, wrap in clingfilm and chill in the refrigerator for 30–60 minutes.

2 Preheat the oven to 190°C/375°F/Gas Mark 5. Line two baking sheets with baking paper.

3 Unwrap the dough and roll out between two sheets of baking paper. Stamp out cookies with a 5-cm/2-inch bell-shaped cutter and put them on the prepared baking sheets, spaced well apart.

4 Bake in the preheated oven for 10–15 minutes, until light golden brown. Leave to cool on the baking sheets for 5–10 minutes, then, using a palette knife, carefully transfer to wire racks to cool completely.

5 Mix together the egg white and lemon juice in a bowl, then gradually beat in the icing sugar until smooth. Leave the cookies on the racks and spread the icing over them. Place a silver ball on the clapper shape at the bottom of the cookie and leave to set completely. When the icing is dry, use the food colouring pens to draw patterns on the cookies.

Date & Lemon
SPIRALS

Makes about 30

- 225 g/8 oz butter, softened
- 175 g/6 oz caster sugar
- 1 egg yolk, lightly beaten
- 1 tsp lemon extract
- 280 g/10 oz plain flour
- pinch of salt
- 280 g/10 oz dried dates, stoned and finely chopped
- 2 tbsp clear lemon blossom honey
- 5 tbsp lemon juice
- 1 tbsp finely grated lemon rind
- 1 tsp ground cinnamon

1 Put the butter and 140 g/5 oz of the sugar into a bowl and mix well with a wooden spoon, then beat in the egg yolk and lemon extract. Sift together the flour and salt into the mixture and stir until thoroughly combined. Shape the dough into a ball, wrap in clingfilm and chill in the refrigerator for 30–60 minutes.

2 Meanwhile, put the dates, honey, lemon juice and lemon rind in a saucepan and stir in 125 ml/4 fl oz of water. Bring to the boil, stirring constantly, then lower the heat and simmer gently, stirring occasionally, for 5 minutes. Remove from the heat and leave to cool, then chill in the refrigerator for 15 minutes.

3 Mix together the cinnamon and remaining sugar in a bowl. Unwrap the dough and roll out between two sheets of baking paper into a 30-cm/12-inch square. Sprinkle the cinnamon and sugar mixture over the dough and roll lightly with the rolling pin. Spread the date mixture evenly over the dough, then roll up like a Swiss roll. Wrap in clingfilm and chill in the refrigerator for 30 minutes.

4 Preheat the oven to 190°C/375°F/Gas Mark 5. Line two baking sheets with baking paper. Unwrap the roll and cut into thin slices with a sharp serrated knife. Put them on the prepared baking sheets, spaced well apart. Bake in the preheated oven for 12–15 minutes, until golden brown. Leave to cool for 5–10 minutes, then transfer to wire racks to cool completely.

Cinnamon
STARS

Makes about 25

- 2 egg whites
- 175 g/6 oz icing sugar,
  plus extra for dusting
- 250 g/9 oz ground hazelnuts,
  roasted
- 1 tbsp ground cinnamon

1 Whisk the egg whites in a clean dry bowl until stiff. Stir in the sugar until thoroughly combined and then continue to whisk until thick and glossy.

2 Remove 40 g/1½ oz of this mixture and set aside. Then fold the hazelnuts and cinnamon into the remaining mixture to make a very stiff dough. Chill in the refrigerator for about an hour.

3 Preheat the oven to 140°C/275°F/Gas Mark 1. Line two baking sheets with baking paper. Roll out the dough to 1 cm/½ inch thick on a surface amply floured with icing sugar.

4 Cut the dough into shapes using a 5-cm/2-inch star-shaped cutter, dusting with icing sugar to prevent sticking. Re-roll as necessary until all mixture is used up.

5 Place the cookies on the prepared baking sheets, spaced well apart, and spread the top of each star with the reserved egg white icing.

6 Bake in the preheated oven for 25 minutes, until the cookies are still white and crisp on top but slightly soft and moist underneath. Turn off the oven and open the oven door to release the heat and dry the cookies out in the oven for 10 more minutes. Transfer to wire racks to cool.

Cinnamon, Cranberry & Blueberry
COOKIES

Makes about 30
- 225 g/8 oz butter, softened
- 140 g/5 oz caster sugar
- 1 egg yolk, lightly beaten
- 2 tsp vanilla extract
- 280 g/10 oz plain flour
- 1 tsp ground cinnamon
- pinch of salt
- 55 g/2 oz dried blueberries
- 55 g/2 oz dried cranberries
- 55 g/2 oz pine kernels, chopped

1 Preheat the oven to 190°C/375°F/Gas Mark 5. Line two baking sheets with baking paper.

2 Put the butter and sugar into a bowl and mix well with a wooden spoon, then beat in the egg yolk and vanilla extract. Sift together the flour, cinnamon and salt into the mixture, add the blueberries and cranberries and stir until thoroughly combined.

3 Spread out the pine kernels in a shallow dish. Scoop up tablespoons of the mixture and roll them into balls. Roll the balls in the pine kernels to coat, then place on the prepared baking sheets, spaced well apart, and flatten slightly.

4 Bake in the preheated oven for 10–15 minutes. Leave to cool on the baking sheets for 5–10 minutes, then, using a palette knife, carefully transfer the cookies to wire racks to cool completely.

Apple Suns &
PEAR STARS

....

Makes about 30

- 225 g/8 oz butter, softened
- 140 g/5 oz caster sugar
- 1 egg yolk, lightly beaten
- 280 g/10 oz plain flour
- pinch of salt
- ½ tsp mixed spice
- 55 g/2 oz dried apple, finely chopped
- ½ tsp ground ginger
- 55 g/2 oz dried pear, finely chopped
- 25 g/1 oz flaked almonds
- 1 egg white, lightly beaten
- demerara sugar, for sprinkling

1 Put the butter and caster sugar into a bowl and mix well with a wooden spoon, then beat in the egg yolk. Sift together the flour and salt into the mixture and stir until thoroughly combined. Transfer half the dough to another bowl.

2 Add the mixed spice and dried apple to one bowl and mix well. Shape into a ball, wrap in clingfilm and chill in the refrigerator for 30–60 minutes. Add the ginger and dried pear to the other bowl and mix well. Shape into a ball, wrap in clingfilm and chill in the refrigerator for 30–60 minutes.

3 Preheat the oven to 190°C/375°F/Gas Mark 5. Line two baking sheets with baking paper.

4 Unwrap the apple-flavoured dough and roll out between two sheets of baking paper to about 3 mm/⅛ inch thick. Stamp out cookies with a sun-shaped cutter and put them on a prepared baking sheet. Repeat with the pear-flavoured dough and stamp out cookies with a star-shaped cutter. Put them on the other prepared baking sheet.

5 Bake in the preheated oven for 5 minutes, then remove the star-shaped cookies from the oven and sprinkle with the flaked almonds. Return to the oven and bake for a further 5–10 minutes. Remove the cookies from the oven but do not turn off the heat. Brush the apple suns with a little egg white and sprinkle with the demerara sugar. Return to the oven for 2–3 minutes. Leave all the cookies to cool for 5–10 minutes, then carefully transfer them to wire racks to cool completely.

White Chocolate &
PLUM COOKIES

Makes about 30

- 225 g/8 oz butter, softened
- 140 g/5 oz caster sugar
- 1 egg yolk, lightly beaten
- 2 tsp vanilla extract
- 225 g/8 oz plain flour
- 55 g/2 oz cocoa powder
- pinch of salt
- 100 g/3½ oz white chocolate, chopped

To decorate

- 55 g/2 oz white chocolate, broken into pieces
- 15 dried plums, halved

1 Put the butter and sugar into a bowl and mix well with a wooden spoon, then beat in the egg yolk and vanilla extract. Sift together the flour, cocoa and salt into the mixture and stir until thoroughly combined. Halve the dough, shape into balls, wrap in clingfilm and chill in the refrigerator for 30–60 minutes.

2 Preheat the oven to 190°C/375°F/Gas Mark 5. Line two baking sheets with baking paper. Unwrap a ball of dough and roll out between two sheets of baking paper to about 3 mm/⅛ inch thick. Stamp out 15 rounds with a plain 5-cm/2-inch cutter and put them on the prepared baking sheets, spaced well apart. Divide the chopped chocolate among the cookies. Roll out the remaining dough between two sheets of baking paper and stamp out rounds with a 6–7-cm/2½–2¾-inch cutter. Place them on top of the first cookies and press the edges together to seal.

3 Bake in the preheated oven for 10–15 minutes, until firm. Leave to cool for 5–10 minutes, then carefully transfer the cookies to wire racks to cool completely. To decorate, melt the chocolate in a heatproof bowl set over a pan of gently simmering water. Remove from the heat and leave to cool slightly. Leave the cookies on the racks. Dip the cut sides of the plums into the melted chocolate and stick them in the middle of the cookies. Spoon the remaining melted chocolate over them and leave to set.

Walnut & Fig
PINWHEELS

Makes about 30
- 225 g/8 oz butter, softened
- 200 g/7 oz caster sugar
- 1 egg yolk, lightly beaten
- 225 g/8 oz plain flour
- pinch of salt
- 55 g/2 oz ground walnuts
- 280 g/10 oz dried figs,
  finely chopped
- 5 tbsp freshly brewed mint tea
- 2 tsp finely chopped fresh mint

1 Put the butter and 140 g/5 oz of the sugar into a bowl and mix well with a wooden spoon, then beat in the egg yolk. Sift together the flour and salt into the mixture, add the ground walnuts and stir until thoroughly combined. Shape the dough into a ball, wrap in clingfilm and chill in the refrigerator for 30–60 minutes.

2 Meanwhile, put the remaining sugar into a saucepan and stir in 125 ml/ 4 fl oz of water, then add the figs, mint tea and chopped mint. Bring to the boil, stirring constantly, until the sugar has dissolved, then lower the heat and simmer gently, stirring occasionally, for 5 minutes. Remove the pan from the heat and leave to cool.

3 Unwrap the dough and roll out between two sheets of baking paper into a 30-cm/12-inch square. Spread the fig filling evenly over the dough, then roll up like a Swiss roll. Wrap in clingfilm and chill in the refrigerator for 30 minutes.

4 Preheat the oven to 190°C/375°F/Gas Mark 5. Line two baking sheets with baking paper. Unwrap the roll and cut into thin slices with a sharp serrated knife. Put the slices on the prepared baking sheets, spaced well apart. Bake in the preheated oven for 10–15 minutes, until golden brown. Leave to cool on the baking sheets for 5–10 minutes, then, using a palette knife, transfer to wire racks to cool completely.

Christmas
TREE COOKIES

Makes 12

- 150 g/5½ oz plain flour, plus extra for dusting
- 1 tsp ground cinnamon
- ½ tsp ground nutmeg
- ½ tsp ground ginger
- 70 g/2½ oz unsalted butter, softened, plus extra for greasing
- 3 tbsp honey

To decorate
- white icing (optional)
- edible coloured balls

1 Sift the flour and spices into a bowl and rub in the butter until the mixture resembles breadcrumbs. Add the honey and mix together well to form a soft dough. Wrap the dough in clingfilm and chill in the refrigerator for 30 minutes.

2 Meanwhile, preheat the oven to 180°C/350°F/Gas Mark 4 and grease two baking sheets. Divide the dough in half. Roll out one piece of dough on a floured work surface to about 5 mm/¼ inch thick. Cut out tree shapes using a cutter or cardboard template. Repeat with the remaining piece of dough.

3 Put the cookies on the prepared baking sheets and, using a skewer, make a hole through the top of each biscuit large enough to thread the ribbon through. Chill in the refrigerator for 15 minutes.

4 Bake in the preheated oven for 10–12 minutes, until golden. Leave to cool on the baking sheets for 5 minutes, then transfer to a wire rack to cool completely. Decorate the trees with white icing and coloured balls, or simply leave them plain, then thread a length of ribbon through each hole and knot. Hang from the Christmas tree.

Stained-glass Window
COOKIES

Makes about 25

- 350 g/12 oz plain flour,
  plus extra for dusting
- pinch of salt
- 1 tsp bicarbonate of soda
- 100 g/3½ oz unsalted butter,
  softened
- 175 g/6 oz caster sugar
- 1 large egg
- 1 tsp vanilla extract
- 4 tbsp golden syrup
- 50 mixed coloured boiled fruit
  sweets (about 250 g/9 oz),
  chopped

1 Sift the flour, salt and bicarbonate of soda into a large bowl, add the butter and rub it in until the mixture resembles breadcrumbs. Stir in the sugar. Place the egg, vanilla extract and golden syrup in a separate bowl and whisk together. Pour the egg into the flour mixture and mix to form a smooth dough. Wrap in clingfilm and chill in the refrigerator for 30 minutes.

2 Preheat the oven to 180°C/350°F/Gas Mark 4. Line two large baking sheets with baking paper. Roll the dough out on a floured work surface to 5 mm/ ¼ inch thick. Use a variety of floured cookie cutter shapes to cut out shapes.

3 Transfer the shapes to the prepared baking sheets and cut out shapes from the centre of the cookies. Fill the holes with the sweets. Using a skewer, make a hole in the top of each cookie.

4 Bake in the preheated oven for 10–12 minutes, or until the sweets are melted. Make sure the holes are still there, and re-pierce if necessary. Leave to cool on the baking sheets until the centres have hardened. When cold, thread thin ribbon through the holes to hang up the cookies.

Spiced
FRUIT COOKIES

Makes about 30
- 225 g/8 oz butter, softened
- 140 g/5 oz caster sugar
- 1 egg yolk, lightly beaten
- 280 g/10 oz plain flour
- ½ tsp mixed spice
- pinch of salt
- 25 g/1 oz dried apple, chopped
- 25 g/1 oz dried pear, chopped
- 25 g/1 oz prunes, chopped
- grated rind of 1 orange

1 Put the butter and sugar into a bowl and mix well with a wooden spoon, then beat in the egg yolk. Sift together the flour, mixed spice and salt into the mixture, add the apple, pear, prunes and orange rind and stir until thoroughly combined. Shape the dough into a log, wrap in clingfilm and chill in the refrigerator for 30–60 minutes.

2 Preheat the oven to 190°C/375°F/Gas Mark 5. Line two baking sheets with baking paper.

3 Unwrap the log and cut it into 5-mm/¼-inch thick slices with a sharp serrated knife. Put them on the prepared baking sheets, spaced well apart.

4 Bake in the preheated oven for 10–15 minutes, until golden brown. Leave to cool on the baking sheets for 5–10 minutes, then, using a palette knife, carefully transfer the cookies to wire racks to cool completely.

GINGER SNAPS

Makes 30

- 350 g/12 oz self-raising flour
- pinch of salt
- 200 g/7 oz caster sugar
- 1 tbsp ground ginger
- 1 tsp bicarbonate of soda
- 125 g/4½ oz butter, plus extra for greasing
- 75 g/2¾ oz golden syrup
- 1 egg, beaten
- 1 tsp grated orange rind

1 Preheat the oven to 160°C/325°F/Gas Mark 3. Grease two baking sheets.

2 Sift together the flour, salt, sugar, ginger and bicarbonate of soda into a large mixing bowl.

3 Heat the butter and golden syrup together in a saucepan over a very low heat until the butter has melted. Remove the pan from the heat and leave to cool slightly, then pour the contents onto the dry ingredients. Add the egg and orange rind and mix thoroughly to form a dough. Using your hands, carefully shape the dough into 30 even-sized balls.

4 Place the balls on the prepared baking sheets, spaced well apart, and flatten slightly with your fingers.

5 Bake in the preheated oven for 15–20 minutes, then carefully transfer to wire racks to cool.

Christmas Tree
DECORATIONS

Makes 20–25

- 225 g/8 oz butter, softened
- 140 g/5 oz caster sugar
- 1 egg yolk, lightly beaten
- 2 tsp vanilla extract
- 280 g/10 oz plain flour
- pinch of salt
- 1 egg white, lightly beaten
- 2 tbsp hundreds-and-thousands
- 400 g/14 oz mixed coloured boiled fruit sweets

1 Put the butter and sugar into a bowl and mix well with a wooden spoon, then beat in the egg yolk and vanilla extract. Sift together the flour and salt into the mixture and stir until thoroughly combined. Halve the dough, shape into balls, wrap in clingfilm and chill in the refrigerator for 30–60 minutes. Preheat the oven to 190°C/375°F/Gas Mark 5. Line two baking sheets with baking paper.

2 Unwrap the dough and roll out between two sheets of baking paper. Stamp out cookies with Christmas tree-shaped cutters and put them on the prepared baking sheets, spaced well apart. Using the end of a large plain piping nozzle, stamp out rounds from each shape and remove them. Make a small hole in the top of each cookie with a skewer so that they can be threaded with ribbon. Brush with egg white and sprinkle with hundreds-and-thousands. Bake in the preheated oven for 7 minutes.

3 Meanwhile, lightly crush the sweets by tapping them with a rolling pin. Unwrap and sort into separate bowls by colour. Remove the cookies from the oven and fill the holes with the crushed sweets. Return to the oven and bake for a further 5–8 minutes, until the cookies are light golden brown and the sweets have melted and filled the holes. Leave to cool. Thread thin ribbon through the holes in the top and hang.

Holly
LEAF COOKIES

Makes 30
- 55 g/2 oz butter, softened,
  plus extra for greasing
- 85 g/3 oz caster sugar
- 1 egg yolk
- ⅛ tsp almond extract
- 115 g/4 oz plain flour,
  plus extra for dusting
- 2 tsp milk
- 85 g/3 oz boiled sweets

1 Cream the butter and sugar together in a bowl until light and fluffy. Beat in the egg yolk and almond extract until smooth and then sift in the flour and add the milk to produce a soft dough. Cover with clingfilm and allow to chill in the refrigerator for 30 minutes.

2 Preheat the oven to 180°C/350°F/Gas Mark 4. Grease two baking sheets. Crush the sweets by tapping them with a rolling pin. Roll out the chilled dough on a lightly floured work surface to 5 mm/¼ inch thick.

3 Use a large holly leaf-shaped cutter to cut out shapes from the dough and then use a smaller holly-shaped cutter to cut out and remove the middle of each larger holly shape.

4 Using a skewer, cut a small hole out of the top of each cookie so they can be threaded with ribbon. Re-knead and re-roll the dough trimmings and cut out until all the dough is used up. Place all the holly shapes on the prepared baking sheets.

5 Divide the crushed boiled sweet pieces evenly to fill the holes in the middle of the cookies. Bake in the preheated oven for 8–10 minutes until the cookies are just turning golden around the edges.

6 When completely cool, transfer the cookies, using a palette knife, to a wire rack. Thread thin ribbon through the holes and hang.

Peach, Pear &
PLUM COOKIES

Makes about 30

- 225 g/8 oz butter, softened
- 140 g/5 oz caster sugar
- 1 egg yolk, lightly beaten
- 2 tsp almond extract
- 280 g/10 oz plain flour
- pinch of salt
- 55 g/2 oz dried peach, finely chopped
- 55 g/2 oz dried pear, finely chopped
- 4 tbsp plum jam

1 Preheat the oven to 190°C/375°F/Gas Mark 5. Line two baking sheets with baking paper.

2 Put the butter and sugar into a bowl and mix well with a wooden spoon, then beat in the egg yolk and almond extract. Sift together the flour and salt into the mixture, add the dried fruit and stir until thoroughly combined.

3 Scoop up tablespoons of the mixture, roll them into balls and place on the prepared baking sheets, spaced well apart. Make a hollow in the centre of each with the dampened handle of a wooden spoon. Fill the hollows with the jam.

4 Bake in the preheated oven for 12–15 minutes, until light golden brown. Leave to cool on the baking sheets for 5–10 minutes, then, using a palette knife, carefully transfer to wire racks to cool completely.

Iced
STARS

Makes 30

- 225 g/8 oz butter, softened
- 140 g/5 oz caster sugar
- 1 egg yolk, lightly beaten
- ½ tsp vanilla extract
- 280 g/10 oz plain flour
- pinch of salt

To decorate

- 200 g/7 oz icing sugar
- 1–2 tbsp warm water
- food colourings
- edible silver and gold balls
- hundreds-and-thousands
- sugar sprinkles
- sugar stars, hearts and flowers
- desiccated coconut

1 Place the butter and caster sugar in a large bowl and beat together until light and fluffy, then beat in the egg yolk and vanilla extract. Sift together the flour and salt into the mixture and stir until thoroughly combined. Halve the dough, shape into balls, wrap in clingfilm and chill in the refrigerator for 30–60 minutes.

2 Preheat the oven to 190°C/375°F/Gas Mark 5. Line two large baking sheets with baking paper.

3 Unwrap the dough and roll out between two sheets of baking paper to about 3 mm/⅛ inch thick. Cut out cookies with a star-shaped cutter and place them on the prepared baking sheets, spaced well apart. Bake in the preheated oven for 10–15 minutes, or until light golden brown. Leave to cool on the baking sheets for 5–10 minutes, then transfer to wire racks to cool completely.

4 To decorate, sift the icing sugar into a bowl and stir in enough warm water until it is the consistency of thick cream. Divide the icing among 3–4 bowls and add a few drops of your chosen food colourings to each. Leave the cookies on the racks and spread the different coloured icings over them to the edges. Arrange silver and gold balls on top and/or sprinkle with hundreds-and-thousands and sugar shapes. If you like, colour desiccated coconut with food colouring in a contrasting colour and sprinkle over the cookies. Leave to set.

Christmas
GIFT COOKIES

Makes about 30
- 225 g/8 oz butter, softened
- 140 g/5 oz caster sugar
- 1 egg yolk, lightly beaten
- 2 tsp orange juice or orange liqueur
- finely grated rind of 1 orange
- 280 g/10 oz plain flour
- pinch of salt

To decorate
- 1 egg white
- 225 g/8 oz icing sugar
- few drops each of 2 food colourings
- edible silver balls

1 Place the butter and caster sugar in a large bowl and beat together until light and fluffy, then beat in the egg yolk, orange juice and grated rind. Sift together the flour and salt into the mixture and stir until combined. Halve the dough, shape into balls, wrap in clingfilm and chill in the refrigerator for 30–60 minutes.

2 Preheat the oven to 190°C/375°F/Gas Mark 5. Line two large baking sheets with baking paper. Unwrap the dough and roll out to 3 mm/⅛ inch thick. Cut out appropriate shapes, such as stars or Christmas trees, with cookie cutters and place them on the baking sheets, spaced well apart. Bake in the preheated oven for 10–15 minutes, or until light golden brown.

3 Leave to cool on the baking sheets for 5–10 minutes, then transfer the cookies to wire racks to cool completely.

4 Leave the cookies on the racks. Put the egg white and icing sugar into a bowl and beat until smooth, adding a little water if necessary. Transfer half the icing to another bowl and colour each bowl with a different colour. Put both icings in piping bags with fine nozzles and use to decorate the cookies and write the initials of the person who will receive the cookies as a gift. Finish with silver balls and leave to set.

Cinnamon
ORANGE CRISPS

Makes about 30

- 225 g/8 oz butter, softened
- 200 g/7 oz caster sugar
- finely grated rind of 1 orange
- 1 egg yolk, lightly beaten
- 4 tsp orange juice
- 280 g/10 oz plain flour
- pinch of salt
- 2 tsp ground cinnamon

1 Place the butter, 140 g/5 oz of the sugar and the orange rind in a large bowl and beat together until light and fluffy, then beat in the egg yolk and 2 teaspoons of the orange juice. Sift together the flour and salt into the mixture and stir until thoroughly combined. Shape the dough into a ball, wrap in clingfilm and chill in the refrigerator for 30–60 minutes.

2 Unwrap the dough and roll out between two sheets of baking paper into a 30-cm/12-inch square. Brush with the remaining orange juice and sprinkle with the remaining sugar and cinnamon. Lightly roll with the rolling pin. Roll up the dough like a Swiss roll. Wrap in clingfilm and chill for 30 minutes.

3 Preheat the oven to 190°C/375°F/Gas Mark 5. Line two large baking sheets with baking paper.

4 Unwrap the dough and cut into thin slices, then place on the prepared baking sheets, spaced well apart. Bake in the preheated oven for 10–12 minutes. Leave to cool for 5–10 minutes, then transfer to wire racks to cool completely.

Christmas
ANGELS

Makes about 25

- 225 g/8 oz butter, softened
- 140 g/5 oz caster sugar
- 1 egg yolk, lightly beaten
- 2 tsp passion fruit pulp
- 280 g/10 oz plain flour
- pinch of salt
- 55 g/2 oz desiccated coconut

To decorate

- 175 g/6 oz icing sugar
- 1–1½ tbsp passion fruit pulp
- edible silver glitter, for sprinkling

1 Put the butter and caster sugar into a bowl and mix well with a wooden spoon, then beat in the egg yolk and passion fruit pulp. Sift together the flour and salt into the mixture, add the coconut and stir until thoroughly combined. Halve the dough, shape into balls, wrap in clingfilm and chill in the refrigerator for 30–60 minutes.

2 Preheat the oven to 190°C/375°F/Gas Mark 5. Line two baking sheets with baking paper.

3 Unwrap the dough and roll out between two sheets of baking paper. Stamp out cookies with a 7-cm/2¾-inch angel-shaped cutter and put them on the prepared baking sheets, spaced well apart.

4 Bake in the preheated oven for 10–15 minutes, until light golden brown. Leave to cool on the baking sheets for 5–10 minutes, then, using a palette knife, carefully transfer to wire racks to cool completely.

5 Sift the icing sugar into a bowl and stir in the passion fruit pulp until the icing has the consistency of thick cream. Leave the cookies on the racks and spread the icing over them. Sprinkle with the edible glitter and leave to set.

Chocolate, Date & Pecan Nut
PINWHEELS

Makes about 30
- 225 g/8 oz butter, softened
- 200 g/7 oz caster sugar
- 1 egg yolk, lightly beaten
- 225 g/8 oz plain flour
- 55 g/2 oz cocoa powder
- pinch of salt
- 100 g/3½ oz pecan nuts,
  finely ground
- 280 g/10 oz dried dates,
  stoned and roughly chopped
- finely grated rind of 1 orange
- 175 ml/6 fl oz orange flower
  water

1 Place the butter and 140 g/5 oz of the sugar in a large bowl and beat together until light and fluffy, then beat in the egg yolk. Sift together the flour, cocoa and salt into the mixture, add the nuts and stir until combined. Halve the dough, shape into balls, wrap in clingfilm and chill in the refrigerator for 30–60 minutes.

2 Meanwhile, place the dates, orange rind, orange flower water and remaining sugar into a saucepan and cook over a low heat, stirring, until the sugar has dissolved. Bring to the boil, then reduce the heat and simmer, for 5 minutes. Pour the mixture into a bowl, cool, then chill.

3 Unwrap the dough and roll out between two sheets of baking paper to rectangles 5 mm/¼ inch thick. Spread the filling over the rectangles and roll up like a Swiss roll. Wrap in the paper and chill in the refrigerator for 30 minutes. Preheat the oven to 190°C/375°F/Gas Mark 5. Line two large baking sheets with baking paper. Unwrap the rolls, cut into 1-cm/½-inch slices and place them on the prepared baking sheets.

4 Bake in the preheated oven for 15–20 minutes, or until golden brown. Leave to cool on the baking sheets for 5–10 minutes, then transfer the cookies to wire racks to cool completely.

German
LEBKUCHEN

Makes 60

- 3 eggs
- 200 g/7 oz caster sugar
- 55 g/2 oz plain flour
- 2 tsp cocoa powder
- 1 tsp ground cinnamon
- ½ tsp ground cardamom
- ¼ tsp ground cloves
- ¼ tsp ground nutmeg
- 175 g/6 oz ground almonds
- 55 g/2 oz mixed peel, finely chopped

To decorate

- 115 g/4 oz plain chocolate, broken into pieces
- 115 g/4 oz white chocolate, broken into pieces
- sugar crystals

1 Preheat the oven to 180°C/350°F/Gas Mark 4. Line several large baking sheets with baking paper. Place the eggs and sugar in a heatproof bowl set over a saucepan of gently simmering water and whisk until thick and foamy. Remove the bowl from the pan and continue to whisk for 2 minutes.

2 Sift the flour, cocoa, cinnamon, cardamom, cloves and nutmeg into the bowl and stir in with the ground almonds and mixed peel. Drop heaped teaspoonfuls of the mixture onto the prepared baking sheets, spreading them gently into smooth mounds.

3 Bake in the preheated oven for 15–20 minutes, or until light brown and slightly soft to the touch. Leave to cool on the baking sheets for 10 minutes, then transfer the cookies to wire racks to cool completely.

4 Place the plain and white chocolate in two separate heatproof bowls, set the bowls over two pans of gently simmering water and heat until melted. Dip half the biscuits in the melted plain chocolate and half in the white chocolate. Sprinkle with sugar crystals and leave to set.

Treacle & Spice
DRIZZLES

Makes about 25

- 200 g/7 oz butter, softened
- 2 tbsp black treacle
- 140 g/5 oz caster sugar
- 1 egg yolk, lightly beaten
- 280 g/10 oz plain flour
- 1 tsp ground cinnamon
- ½ tsp grated nutmeg
- ½ tsp ground cloves
- pinch of salt
- 2 tbsp chopped walnuts

To decorate

- 115 g/4 oz icing sugar
- 1 tbsp hot water
- a few drops of yellow food colouring
- a few drops of pink food colouring

1 Put the butter, treacle and caster sugar into a bowl and mix well with a wooden spoon, then beat in the egg yolk. Sift together the flour, cinnamon, nutmeg, cloves and salt into the mixture, add the walnuts and stir until thoroughly combined. Halve the dough, shape into balls, wrap in clingfilm and chill in the refrigerator for 30–60 minutes.

2 Preheat the oven to 190°C/375°F/Gas Mark 5. Line two baking sheets with baking paper.

3 Unwrap the dough and roll out between two sheets of baking paper to about 5 mm/¼ inch thick. Stamp out rounds with a 6-cm/2½-inch fluted cutter and put them on the prepared baking sheets.

4 Bake in the preheated oven for 10–15 minutes, until firm. Leave to cool on the baking sheets for 5–10 minutes, then, using a palette knife, carefully transfer the cookies to wire racks to cool completely.

5 For the icing, sift the icing sugar into a bowl, then gradually stir in the hot water until the icing has the consistency of thick cream. Spoon half the icing into another bowl and stir a few drops of yellow food colouring into one bowl and a few drops of pink food colouring into the other. Leave the cookies on the racks and, using teaspoons, drizzle the yellow icing over them in one direction and the pink icing over them at right angles. Leave to set.

Silver
STAR COOKIES

Makes 36

- 175 g/6 oz plain flour, plus extra for dusting
- 1 tsp ground cinnamon
- 1 tsp ground ginger
- 90 g/3¼ oz butter, softened
- 85 g/3 oz soft light brown sugar
- finely grated rind of 1 orange
- 1 egg, lightly beaten

To decorate

- 200 g/7 oz icing sugar
- 3–4 tsp cold water
- edible silver cake sparkles
- edible silver balls

1 Preheat the oven to 180°C/350°F/Gas Mark 4. Line several large baking sheets with baking paper.

2 Sift the flour, cinnamon and ginger into a large bowl. Add the butter and rub it in with your fingertips until the mixture resembles fine breadcrumbs. Stir the brown sugar and orange rind into the mixture, add the egg and mix together to form a soft dough.

3 Roll the mixture out thinly to about 5 mm/¼ inch thick on a lightly floured work surface. Cut out shapes with a 6.5-cm/2½-inch snowflake- or star-shaped cutter and place on the prepared baking sheets.

4 Bake in the preheated oven for 10–15 minutes, or until golden brown. Leave to cool on the baking sheets for 2–3 minutes, then transfer the cookies to a wire rack and leave to cool completely.

5 To make the icing, sift the icing sugar into a large bowl and add enough cold water to make a smooth, thick icing. Spread a little on each cookie and then sprinkle with sparkles and silver balls.

Christmas Stocking
COOKIES

Makes 30

- 100 g/3½ oz butter, plus extra for greasing
- 55 g/2 oz caster sugar
- 1 egg, beaten
- finely grated rind and juice of 1 lemon
- 225 g/8 oz plain flour, plus extra for dusting

- 25 g/1 oz cornflour, plus extra for dusting
- ½ tsp baking powder
- 1 tbsp mixed spice

To decorate
- 250 g/9 oz ready-to-roll fondant icing

- glycerine-based red and green food colouring
- 280 g/10 oz icing sugar
- 1 egg white
- ½ tsp glycerine

1 Beat together the butter and caster sugar in a bowl with a whisk until creamy. Then gradually beat in the egg and lemon rind. Sift together the flour, cornflour, baking powder and mixed spice into the mixture and stir to combine thoroughly into a soft dough. Wrap in clingfilm and chill in the refrigerator for 30 minutes.

2 Preheat the oven to 180°C/350°F/Gas Mark 4. Grease two baking sheets. Roll out on a lightly floured work surface to 5 mm/¼ inch thick. Using a Christmas stocking-shaped cutter, cut out shapes from the dough and place on the prepared baking sheets. Re-knead and re-roll trimmings and cut out until all the dough is used up. Bake in the preheated oven for 15 minutes, until just golden. Allow to cool for 5 minutes, before transferring to a wire rack to cool.

3 Mix the green colouring into 25 g/1 oz fondant icing, adding a little icing sugar until well blended. Cover to prevent drying out. Repeat with remaining fondant icing and the red food colouring. Roll out the green fondant icing as thinly as possible on a surface lightly dusted in cornflour and cut out shapes using a small holly-leaf cutter. Set aside. Roll out the red fondant icing, again as thinly as possible. Cut out shapes using the Christmas stocking-shaped cutter. Stick each stocking to the cookie by using a little lemon juice.

4 Whisk together the remaining icing sugar, egg white and glycerine for 5 minutes with an electric whisk until stiff and glossy. Slacken the mixture if needed with a little lemon juice to make it thick, but still possible to pipe. Fill a piping bag, fitted with a small star-shaped nozzle, with this icing sugar mixture. Pipe rows of stars to form a furry cuff on each stocking. Stick a holly-leaf shape into the piped icing on each cookie. Leave to set.

217

It's All Over... Until
NEXT YEAR!

Christmas doesn't end on Boxing Day. In fact, one of the lovely things about Christmas is that the traditional celebrations continue into the New Year... right up until January 5th when the decorations finally have to come down. In many ways, Christmas is unique in that the main event actually comes in the middle of the celebrations, as opposed to at the climax of them.

Having said that, of course, things do start to wind down after the 25th. The turkey will slowly disappear into soup and sandwiches, the cookies, cakes, sweets and treats will gradually be consumed, and the last of the Christmas parties will morph into the first of the New Year's gatherings.

All of which makes it the perfect time to prepare for next year! As detailed in the Introduction, when the time does come to take down the decorations, organised and methodical storing will make things run smoother next year. And a certain ruthlessness won't hurt either – as you pack away, repair any damaged decorations you can't bear to lose and bin those that are beyond repair. Make a list now of any replacements you will need and be sure to grab them when they're going cheap in January. You can save a fortune by going around the shops in the sales after Christmas and buying up discounted cards, decorations, gifts and packaging.

It's also a good time to prepare next year's cards. As well as catching the last of the bargains from the card shops, making your own now will help keep a little more seasonal spirit going into the very last days of December. Why not try making these snowmen cards and store them away for next year? For this project, you will need a pencil, craft knife, steel-edged ruler, cutting mat, bone folder or scoring tool, permanent black marker pen, wool needle, hole punch, double-sided tape and superglue.

218

Christmas Card Snowmen

Materials

- 300 gsm white card
- scrap card
- roll of pewter lightweight metal foil
- 90 gsm white paper
- thick tracing paper
  11.5 cm/4⅜ inches square
- 2 ready-made embossed snowflakes,
  about 4.5 cm/1¾ inches in diameter
- craft equipment (see bottom of page 218)

1 Using a craft knife and a steel-edged ruler on a cutting mat, cut a piece of the white card 12.5 x 25 cm/4¾ x 10 inches. Score down the centre with a bone folder or a scoring tool and fold in half. Copy the template on page 220 on a photocopier and cut out. Draw around the template on to scrap card and cut out with a craft knife and steel-edged ruler on a cutting mat. Draw around the template three times on to the foil using the marker pen.

2 Cut the snowmen out with the craft knife, but slightly change each one to give them individual character. For example, make the first snowman's hat taller, the second one's body larger and the third one's face a different shape.

3 Cut a strip of pewter foil 7 mm x 11.5 cm/⅜ x 4⅜ inches. Dab it all over with the wool needle to create texture. Punch about 24 dots from the white paper.

4 Attach the pewter strip about 7 mm/¼ inch from the bottom of the tracing paper with double-sided tape. Place double-sided tape on the reverse of the tracing paper and pewter strip, and attach to the folded card, positioning it centrally.

5 Carefully lift the tracing paper to attach the embossed snowflakes to the card with double-sided tape. Add a few paper dots, ensuring that there are two in either top corner. Place a droplet of superglue on each of these corner dots to fasten the tracing paper securely. Stick another two paper dots to the tracing paper to hide the glue marks.

6 Attach the snowmen at different angles with double-sided tape, ensuring that they are butted up against the pewter strip. Add the remaining paper dots around the snowmen.

Christmas Craft Templates

Christmas
Snowflake Card
(enlarge by 200%)

Christmas Card
Snowman (no need
to enlarge)

Country-style
Garland
(enlarge by
200%)

Reindeer
Tea-light Box
(enlarge by
400%)

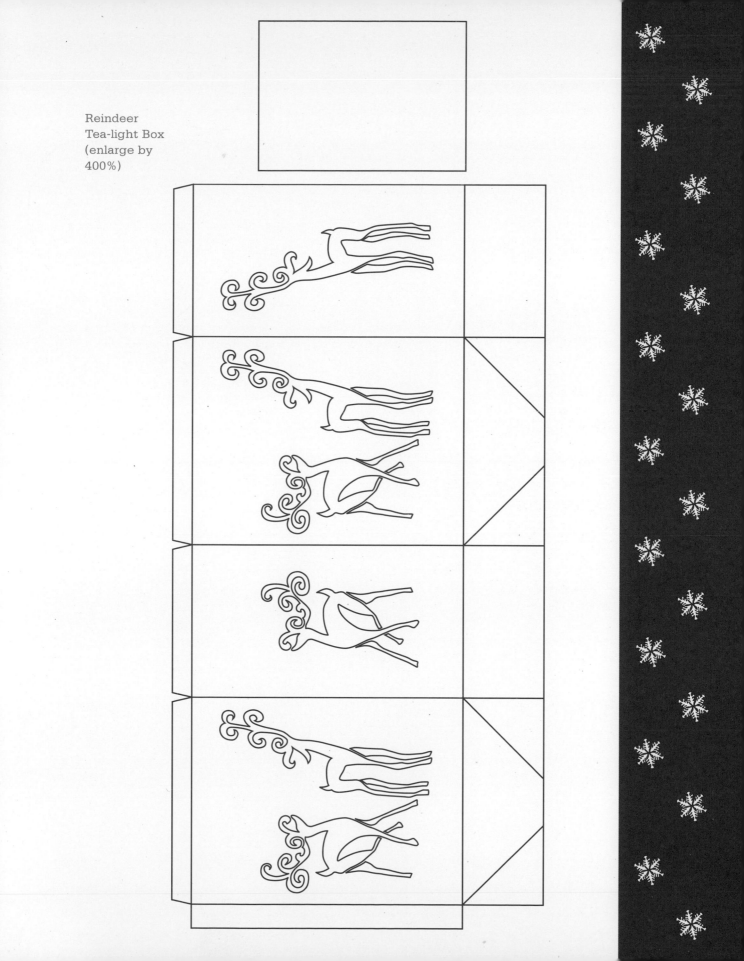